Spirituality for Everyday Life

with Ronald Rolheiser

Living in the Sacred

Trish Sullivan Vanni

RENEW
INTERNATIONAL

NIHIL OBSTAT

Reverend Monsignor Gerard McCarren, S.T.D.
Censor Librorum

IMPRIMATUR

Most Reverend John J. Myers, J.C.D., D.D.
Archbishop of Newark

Cover design: Ruth Markworth
Text design: James F. Brisson
Text illustration: Marion C. Honors, CSJ

ISBN: 978-1-62063-104-1

RENEW International
1232 George Street
Plainfield, NJ 07062-1717
To order, call 1-888-433-3221
www.renewintl.org

Contents

CONTENTS

With Deep Gratitude

WE ARE DEEPLY GRATEFUL to Ronald Rolheiser, OMI, for graciously making available to RENEW selections from his book *Sacred Fire* to create the heart of this faith-sharing resource. Without his generosity and support, *Living in the Sacred* would not have come to fruition.

Presenting
RENEW International

L IVING IN THE SACRED is a 12-session process of spiritual and pastoral renewal developed by RENEW International. It is the second part of a two-part series, *Spirituality for Everyday Life with Ronald Rolheiser.*

The RENEW process, both parish-based and diocese-wide, was first developed and implemented in the Archdiocese of Newark, New Jersey. Its success there led other dioceses, in the United States and in other countries, to bring RENEW to their people and parish communities. In the three decades since its vibrant beginnings, RENEW International has touched the lives of 25 million people in over 170 dioceses in the United States, Canada, and 23 countries throughout the world.

RENEW International has grown organically from its original single RENEW process. Materials and training have been inculturated and made available in over 40 languages. We have added specific pastoral outreach to campuses and to young adults in their 20s and 30s. We have incorporated prison ministry and provided resources for the visually impaired.

The very core of all of these processes remains the same: to help people become better hearers and doers of the Word of God. We do this by encouraging and supporting the formation of small communities who gather prayerfully to reflect on and share the Word of God, to make better connections between faith and life, and to live their faith more concretely in family, work, and community life.

As a not-for-profit organization, our pastoral outreach is sustained in part from the sales of our publications and resources, and the stipends we receive for the services provided to parishes and dioceses. However, our priority is always to serve all parishes who desire to renew their faith and build the Church, regardless of their economic situation. We have been able to fulfill this mission not only in the inner city and rural areas in the United States, but also in the developing world, especially Latin America and Africa, thanks to donations and charitable funding.

As you meet in your small group, we invite you to take a few moments to imagine the great invisible network of others, here in the United States and on the other continents. They gather, as you do, in small Christian communities, around the Word of God present in the Scripture, striving to hear and act upon that Word.

Keep them in your prayer: a prayer of thanksgiving for the many graces we have experienced; a prayer that the Spirit will guide all of us as we strive to recognize that we are "living in the sacred."

Foreword

FOR MORE THAN 35 YEARS, RENEW International has been the catalyst in the spiritual renewal of Catholic parishes and dioceses. Through the formation of small groups, people gather weekly—often in each other's homes—to pray, read Scripture and reflections on various topics, share faith, and develop plans to put their faith into action. I was delighted when Sr. Terry Rickard, OP, RENEW's president and executive director, called me to ask if I would be interested in working with RENEW on a small-group resource based on my recently published book, *Sacred Fire: A Vision for a Deeper Human and Christian Maturity*.

I recalled how several years earlier, Msgr. Thomas Kleissler, co-founder of RENEW, along with several RENEW staff members, had visited me in Toronto to discuss a similar small-group resource based on my books, *The Holy Longing* and *The Shattered Lantern*. *Longing for the Holy*, the resource that resulted from that conversation, took many of the ideas and insights about Christian spirituality that I shared in these books and put them into the familiar format that RENEW uses to engage small groups in faith sharing. RENEW matched up my themes with passages from Scripture, wrote reflections and questions for faith sharing, and made suggestions for people to put their faith into action.

FOREWORD

In these small-group gatherings, the deep sharing of thoughts, and feelings, and ways in which participants had strived to become better disciples of Christ touched many. I was very pleased then to see the content of my work made available in the format that RENEW has made popular, and I could not be happier to see *Living in the Sacred*, based on *Sacred Fire*, made available now.

In *Sacred Fire*, I invite readers to explore the second of what I have described as the three stages of Christian discipleship—essential, mature, and radical. Essential discipleship, which usually commences at puberty, and radical discipleship, which occurs as we approach death, are described in the introduction to this book.

Mature discipleship, the subject of this volume, involves us in what I call the struggle to give our lives away. People usually undertake this search when they are in their twenties or thirties, although some may not engage in it until later in life. To put it simply, this stage begins when we become more concerned with the needs and wellbeing of others than we are with our own lives. For most of us, the commitments we have made—to spouses, children, communities, churches—will shape the remainder of our adult lives, and our continuing task will be to determine how we can give our lives away more purely and more generously.

I hope, through RENEW's ministry, to bring my work in this aspect of spirituality to people in parishes who will have the opportunity to gather and share in small groups so that they might grow into mature discipleship!

Ronald Rolheiser, OMI

Living
in the
Sacred

Introduction

IN *SACRED FIRE*, THE BELOVED SPIRITUAL WRITER Ronald Rolheiser, OMI explores what it means to grow across the course of a lifetime into a more prayerful, mature disciple of Jesus Christ. When Fr. Rolheiser writes of that process he uses the image of wine. Like a fine wine, we are not ripe, ready, and at our fullness early in the process of our development as human persons. We need time to ferment, to age and mellow, before we can truly plumb the spiritual depths that are inherent in each of us.

Living in the Sacred, which is based on Fr. Rolheiser's book *Sacred Fire*, becomes the second book in a two-part series from RENEW International. The first, *Longing for the Holy*, is based on his book *The Holy Longing*.

As we get older, life itself provides the crucible in which we have opportunities to become deeper and wiser. We experience this ourselves and witness it in the lives of the people around us. We also read about it in the lives of important personalities. In the biblical Book of Samuel, for example, we read that as Samuel worked in the Temple he "continued to grow both in stature and in favor with the Lord and with the people." The life of Jesus illustrates that growth comes with age and experience. In the Gospel of Luke we are told that after the energetic adolescent adventure in which Jesus left his parents and lingered in the Temple in Jerusalem, "Jesus increased in wisdom and in years, and in divine and human favor" (Luke 2:52). If the Messiah himself had to go through this process, no wonder that we must, too!

While happy, upbeat experiences can provide some degree of change and learning for each of us, Fr. Rolheiser notes that our deepest spiritual changes usually emerge from the fire of life's struggles. We are dealt with a crushing loss, such as the death of a cherished family member or friend. We face a health crisis, and our once vital body is now an impediment in our lives. We discover that the things we thought would make us happy— the job, the house, the perfect family—are not enough to fill a chronic ache or longing within us.

Discipleship and the Stages of Our Lives

While we may be growing and changing until our last breath, the struggles we face are not always the same. Fr. Rolheiser suggests that we can divide our spiritual development into three life chapters: Essential Discipleship, Mature or Generative Discipleship, and Radical Discipleship. Some people will journey through all three stages; others will not.

Essential Discipleship

The first phase, Essential Discipleship, is the period in which we are working to build our lives and become adults. We might call it the "getting our act together" period. It begins at our birth, but it peaks as we leave our homes and families and set out on our own to create lives for ourselves.

In this stage of discipleship, we face fundamental life questions: Who am I? Who loves me? With whom should I partner to build a future? What is my vocation in life, or at least, what kind of job do I want to do? Where do I want to settle down?

Some people move very smoothly through this stage. They reach their late teens and early twenties and move with relative ease into new settings such as college, a job, or military service. Others struggle with developing in Essential Discipleship well into their thirties, forties, and fifties—if not their entire lives.

If you ask people about the season of Essential Discipleship, they can point to moments of struggle that changed them or that illuminated the path before them. They have not been afraid to hit the mats with the Angel of the Lord in the manner of Jacob in the Bible (Genesis 32:22-31). These wrestling matches are often filled with energy and fraught with meaning.

In this season of life, we also come to terms with our sexual selves and learn to tame and channel the drives of our sexuality. The events that color this first stage often involve facing an inherent restlessness or a struggle for meaning. We might find ourselves battling with loneliness or depression. With each experience, we are working to carve out a healthy sense of personal identity. We long for a time when life was not quite so complex, or we might find ourselves hungering for new experiences.

In movies like *Back to the Future* and *Freaky Friday*, Hollywood painted nostalgic pictures of people who returned to their adolescent or teenage years for more fun and frolic. Most people's response to the prospect of being 13, 17, or 20 again might be more like that of a character in the movie *Big*. When the female protagonist is offered an opportunity to become a teen for a second time and accompany her love back home to late adolescence, she smiles and happily declines. Reliving all of those life lessons holds little appeal!

Toward the end of Essential Discipleship, we may find ourselves addressing new challenges and questions. We thought that after we climbed the mountain of accomplishment we could sit back and enjoy the view. Instead, we may be gripped by angst, disappointment, resentment, and exhaustion. At this point, we might find ourselves singing along with Peggy Lee, "Is that all there is?"

Jesus Meets Us Where We Are

Jesus meets us differently at different points in the journey of discipleship. Have you noticed that the parables in the Gospels have resonated differently with you at various stages of your life, or that the character in the story with whom you identify has changed?

Take, for example, the parable of the Prodigal Son. Early in the experience of Essential Discipleship, we might most readily identify with the demanding younger son who defies social convention and the rules of obedience to obtain his share of the family fortune so he can strike out on his own and have the adventures for which he longs.

Toward the end of Essential Discipleship, we might feel more compassion for the older son. How is this scenario fair? Why, we might ask, should someone who "plays by the rules" be second banana to someone who flaunted every value the family and community held dear?

In many ways, both sons in the parable are moving into a new phase of spiritual maturity. Each is called to move past his self-centered point of view and begin looking outside himself to the bigger picture. Each is called to move out of Essential Discipleship into the second stage, Mature Discipleship.

Generative or Mature Discipleship

Once we have done the work of Essential Discipleship, we enter what Fr. Rolheiser calls *Generative* or *Mature Discipleship*. As mature disciples, our gaze shifts; we are not looking inward and focusing on ourselves. Instead, we begin looking outward.

As Mature Disciples, we are less concerned with our own little worlds and more concerned with the world at large. We ask ourselves, "What am I called to do to make the world a better place?" We become more altruistic. We find ourselves being more generous. We call ourselves to deeper levels of faithfulness and action. We become conscious of making and keeping commitments that matter. In other words, we start giving away the "self" we have created during the phase of Essential Discipleship.

If in the Essential Discipleship stage we are all about building our lives, in the generative or mature stage of discipleship, we are all about giving our lives away. As we will see in Session 1, the father in the parable just mentioned represents, in many ways, the Mature Disciple.

Radical Discipleship

In Radical Discipleship, we recognize that we are no longer the builders and leaders that we were in the earlier phases of our lives. We have fully formed and lived in an identity, and that identity is no longer as important in our lives.

In Radical Discipleship, our questions change. We are no longer focused on the task of contributing, of making a difference. Our horizon is now the end of life. We begin to inquire into how our departure from this life will have the greatest impact. We

ask, "How can I live so that my death will be an optimal blessing for my family, my Church, and the world?"

Looking at Jesus, we see a life lived and a death offered for all. Jesus lived for us, and he died for us, and Fr. Rolheiser suggests that these are two different "movements":

> Like Jesus, we too are meant to give our lives away in generosity and selflessness, but we are also meant to give our deaths away, not just at the moment of our deaths, but in a whole process of leaving this planet in such a way that our diminishment and death is our final, and perhaps greatest, gift to the world. Needless to say that's not easy. Walking in discipleship behind the master will require that we too sweat blood and feel "a stone's throw" from everybody. This struggle, to give our deaths away, constitutes Radical Discipleship.

This faith-sharing book, *Living in the Sacred,* will explore the second phase of discipleship, the mature or generative phase.

A Note about Time and the Journey

The ancient Greeks had two words to describe time: *chronos* and *kairos*. We get the word "chronology" from the former. Chronos represented clock time—the measurable hours, minutes and seconds. *Kairos* represents moments—those intense experiences that crystalize time or even give us a sense of moving beyond time. In our Catholic tradition, we use the word *kairos* to describe spiritual time and experience.

Fr. Rolheiser's three phases of discipleship are not rigidly bracketed into chronological age groups. The phases of discipleship offered to us by Fr. Rolheiser are better thought of as happening in *kairological* not chronological time. Some people's life experiences move them quickly through Essential Discipleship to Generative Discipleship. For example, a highly-regarded teacher of preaching was once asked if teens could preach the

Gospel. Her answer was, "They could if they have experienced the Paschal Mystery"—in other words, if in their own lives they have come to know and experience suffering, death, and resurrection. If they have reached that *Kairos*, that moment in their lives, they may be mature disciples although they are young chronologically.

As mentioned earlier, many people never move past Essential Discipleship no matter how old they get. They face death suffering from "scruples" and fear, because they have never been able to turn their gaze outward.

As You Begin...

Your small group may have already spent time exploring the category of Essential Discipleship with *Longing for the Holy*, a faith-sharing resource from RENEW International inspired by Fr. Rolheiser's book *The Holy Longing*. You looked in depth at the great mysteries of Christian faith. You used prayer and reflection to deepen your understanding in new and important ways.

If your group has not used *Longing for the Holy*, we hope that the detail in this introduction has provided a framework in which to join in the conversation

Living in the Sacred invites you to explore the mature or generative phase of discipleship. It will help you look in depth at what it means to have a mature spiritual life.

Like *Longing for the Holy*, it will offer scripture passages, exemplars from Christian history, personal reflections, sharing questions, examples of faith-based action, and prayer.

You will be invited to pray and reflect before you gather, and to join in a short ritual to set the stage at the beginning of each session. Jesus told his disciples and us, "Where two or three are gathered together in my name, there I am in the midst of them" (Matthew 18:20). Jesus Christ, invited into your gathering, is part of your group, and ready to work within the hearts and minds of you who are taking this journey together.

What to Expect at Each Gathering

After the group gathers and is seated, participants, beginning with the leader, will introduce themselves.

Personal Sharing

"How am I right now?" or "What good news would I like to share?"

You will be invited to share with your group the answer to either of the questions above. Each person should be brief and honest. While this is not only a support group, it is good to let people know about the struggles you may be experiencing in your spiritual life or the gratitude that you are presenting to God in your prayer: "My teen son is still causing a lot of stress in our household due to his attitude," or "They announced layoffs at my firm, and I find myself worrying about the future," or "My mother's biopsy was negative, and I'm so grateful and relieved." Maybe your answer will simply be, "I'm here, and I'm glad I'm giving myself this time with you and with God."

Sharing the Good News

Starting with the second session, you will have an opportunity to share with your group what happened in your life as a consequence of the previous session. It may be that you incorporated a new spiritual practice into your weekly routine. It may be that you found a way to deepen an existing personal relationship or begin a relationship with someone you perceive as neglected or lonely. If you let the process into your heart and mind, you will find the word of God opening you up, challenging you, and filling you in new ways.

Lifting Our Hearts

...in Song

St. Augustine said that whoever sings prays twice. As part of centering your attention, you will listen to or sing a song related to the content of the session. Your group leader will prepare this for you. Each session offers suggestions, and you may find yourself seeking out one or more of the songs to accompany you during the week. Music allows us to enter even more deeply into our connection with God in the moment.

...in the Quiet

You will also be invited to spend a few minutes in silence. Being quiet is something of a radical act in a society that is as plugged in as ours. Taking a few deep breaths not only centers us in our bodies but allows us to release the tension of the day and be fully present.

...in the Word

Your group members will take turns reading passages from Scripture each week. When it is your turn, read aloud in a way that allows your listeners to drink in what you are saying. Read slowly. Read with emphasis that underscores what is important but without a theatricality that would distract them from what you are saying. When you are done, pause for a short time. Allow yourself—and your group members—to absorb what you have just heard.

... in Prayer

Your group will close this time of "Lifting Our Hearts" with a short prayer, but all of your time together—sharing faith, reading together—is a prayer designed to connect you more with Jesus Christ and one another.

Our Companion on the Journey

Each session includes both a quote and a biographical sketch of one of the great Christian witnesses of our tradition. We believe that we are surrounded by a "cloud of witnesses" (Hebrews 12:1). These people are exemplars to us. Their lives illuminate what it means to be a disciple of Jesus Christ and to live in a way that reflects "the way and the truth and the life" (John 14:6).

Encountering Wisdom for Life

Take some time to read and review the session in advance. When you are finished, pause to consider what you have read. You may find that you have new insights or want to underline or highlight what stood out for you as you read.

Sharing Our Faith

At this point in your gathering, you'll begin sharing your responses to the questions in the *Living in the Sacred* session. Have a member of your group read the question aloud. Group members respond after reflecting on the question for a few moments. Allow each person who wishes to share. Be aware that some people are introverted, and that silence may allow someone who feels reticent to speak to begin doing so. Listen attentively to each other, but avoid evaluating and judging. You may find that your responses are very different from those of others. The Spirit moves in each of us in different ways. Being open to each other and supporting each other can be among the greatest gifts your group will experience.

Living the Good News

Each time you meet, you will have the option to choose an individual or a collective action you will take in response to that session's content. You should choose something that will have meaning within the context of your life and commitments. Share this with the group. If you decide on a collective action, determine who will take responsibility for various aspects of your plan. Examples of such actions are included in each session.

As each session draws to a close, you will be asked to write in a journal or notebook. This is time for you to reflect on where you see the Spirit of God moving you. What did the prayer inspire in you? The Scripture? The reflections of the others in your group? The individual or collective action you identified?

Closing Prayer

You will complete your time together with a closing prayer. Intercessory prayers, like those at Mass, that address our personal or group needs and longings are appropriate, as are prayers of thanksgiving and praise. You do not need to script these; simply ask people to share from the heart.

Looking Ahead

Remember: Your group experience is made richer when you come to it prepared. Set aside time to read and prayerfully reflect on the next session in the days ahead in preparation for the time you meet again.

Informal Gathering

Your group time is structured so that you can have the best possible experience. Many groups like to close their gathering with informal time to connect and catch up. Your group may have members you don't know well yet, and having conversation over snacks and beverages can deepen both new and old connections.

Here is a sample timeline for your *Living in the Sacred* session:

1. **Sharing*** "How am I feeling right now?" or "What good news would I like to share?"	**20 min.**
2. **Lifting Our Hearts** ... in Song ... in the Quiet ... in the Word ... in Prayer	**20 min.**
3. **Our Companion on the Journey**	**5 min.**
4. **Encountering Wisdom for Life**	**10 min.**
5. **Sharing Our Faith**	**30 min.**
6. **Living the Good News**	**10 min.**
7. **Closing Prayer/Looking Ahead**	**10 min.**
8. **Informal Gathering**	**15 min.**

*In Session 1, during the time for Sharing, briefly introduce yourself. You will begin Sharing the Good News during Session 2.

Becoming accustomed to a simple pattern such as this frees us from always having to figure out what comes next. It allows us to simply sink into the deeper parts of ourselves and listen together with true attentiveness to God's gracious stirrings in our lives.

A Note for Small Community Leaders

Song suggestions may be found on the CD Songs for *Longing for the Holy* available from RENEW International. Visit www.renewintl.org/spiritualityCD.

About the Author

Trish Sullivan Vanni is a consultant to parishes, dioceses, and ministry professional associations in the areas of formation, vision casting, and mission development. She has written magazine articles and books published for the Catholic community. Trish received a master of divinity degree at St. John's University in Collegeville, Minnesota, and an interdisciplinary Ph.D. in Roman Catholic ecclesiology and organizational leadership theory at the Graduate Theological Union in Berkeley, California. She lives in Eden Prairie, Minnesota, with her sculptor husband, Peter, and her three children.

☙ Simply put, the invitations that come to us from Scripture, particularly from Jesus, meet us in very different ways at different times in our lives. We hear them in one way when we are young, in another in midlife, and in still quite a different way when we are old and facing death. Moreover, not all of Jesus' invitations ask for the same level of response at a given time in our lives. Some of his challenges are meant to help bring us to basic conversion, some are meant to deepen that conversion, and still others are meant to take that conversion to its full term and make us full saints. At one stage of our lives, Jesus calls us to give up something for God, at another stage he calls us to give up everything. Sometimes Jesus invites us to small conversions, and sometimes he invites us to martyrdom. Looking at the challenges of Jesus, we see that one size does not fit all!

Sacred Fire, page 6

The Movement toward Mature Discipleship

The Struggle to Give Our Lives Away

Sharing

Briefly share on one of the following questions:

"How am I right now?" or
"What good news would I like to share?"

Lifting Our Hearts

... in Song

Play or sing the following song or another song of your choosing:

"Weave One Heart"

... in the Quiet

Pause for a few moments of silence, and allow yourself to more deeply embrace the presence of God.

... in the Word

Read aloud Luke 15:11-32

The Parable of the Prodigal Son

As the reader proclaims the sacred text, allow yourself to ponder a word, a phrase, a question, or a feeling that rises up from within you. Reflect on this in silence; when you are invited, briefly share it aloud with the group.

(If no one wishes to speak, simply allow the group to be enveloped in the silence, and allow the reflection to continue for a few more moments.)

... in Prayer

> Loving God,
> like a shepherd who gathers his flock,
> carrying the lambs in his arms,
> you gather us now.
> Be with us in our journey of deepening our
>   discipleship.
> In our time together,
> help us come to know you more deeply.
> Help us listen for your voice and walk in your ways,
> so that wherever we go,
> people come to love you more fully.
> We pray this in the name of Jesus. Amen.

Our Companion on the Journey

St. John of the Cross

"Those desiring to climb to the summit of the mount in
    order to become an altar for the offering of a sacrifice
of pure love and praise and reverence to God must first
accomplish these three tasks perfectly. First, they must
    cast out strange gods, all alien affections and attach-
ments. Second, by denying these appetites and repent-
ing of them—through the dark night of the senses—they

must purify themselves of the residue. Third, in order to reach the top of this high mount, their garments must be changed. By means of the first two works, God will substitute new garments for the old. The soul will be clothed in a new understanding of God in God (through removal of the old understanding) and in a new love of God in God, once the will is stripped of all the old cravings and satisfactions. And God will vest the soul with new knowledge when the other old ideas and images are cast aside [Colossians 3:9]."

St. John of the Cross

S T. JOHN OF THE CROSS, was born Juan de Yepes y Alvarez in 1542 near Ávila, Spain. His father died when the boy was seven. Juan's mother sent Juan and his brother to a school for poor children. Juan was deeply affected by the transformation in his brother, Francisco, from a dandy to a person focused on serving people who were poor.

Juan worked at a hospital, studied under the newly founded Jesuits, and then entered the Carmelite order as John of St. Matthias. After ordination at age 25, he met the Carmelite Teresa of Ávila. She convinced him to help her restore the "Primitive Rule" of 1209 which required daily chanting of the *Divine Office*, devotional reading, study, participation in Mass, and periods of solitude and silence. John established a friary for men, the first to adhere to these principles. At that time, he changed his name to John of the Cross.

To help him experience the suffering Jesus,

John wore a hair shirt, fasted, and slept on a wooden board in a small cubicle. Sometime between 1574 and 1577, John had a vision of the crucified Christ, which he recreated in a drawing that still exists, and heard God telling him that he would be part of bringing greater perfection to religious life.

In 1577, Carmelites who opposed the reforms of Teresa imprisoned John. He was tried and convicted by a court of friars and subjected to public lashing, confinement in a cell barely large enough for his body, and a sparse diet. He escaped the following year.

John established eight more Carmelite monasteries. He died in 1591.

Like other saints of the Church, John struggled with periods in which he did not feel the presence of God. His most famous poem, *The Dark Night of the Soul*, describes the path of reaching spiritual maturity. In it, hardship and separation are not seen as problems but as natural stages of achieving union with God.

After the initial "honeymoons" of life—as newlyweds, newly-professed members of religious orders, or new employees—the initial luster and excitement may wear off. We can find ourselves bored, frustrated, or unstimulated. John's great works have endured over centuries because they offer readers a path of return to intimate, passionate communion with God, even at times of duress. John's life demonstrates the journey to becoming a mature disciple of Jesus Christ.

Encountering Wisdom for Life

I F THE TWO BROTHERS in the "Prodigal Son" parable represent two stages in essential discipleship, in many ways the father—the unreasonably generous, forgiving parent—is a wonderful representation of Mature Discipleship.

In effect, the younger son has told the father, "You are dead to me." But the father has defied social convention by meeting his son's demands. He has seen his hard-earned wealth squandered. He has lost his child to the drives of youth. And yet he offers forgiveness, love, and generosity when his son returns. The father's focus is not on himself but on those around him–including his wayward child and his suffering older son. He is the mature or generative disciple.

We know that we have crossed into this phase when we realize that we are living more for others than for ourselves. This may happen as we care for our spouses and our children, or in the ways we live our professional lives or serve the communities of which we are a part. Most people begin moving to mature discipleship in their 20s or 30s; for some it can take longer or never happen at all.

Moving to Mature Discipleship

How exactly do we move to mature discipleship? Fr. Rolheiser offers four focal points of practice. Each is grounded in the teaching of Jesus.

Private prayer and private integrity

We must have an intimate relationship with Jesus if we are to follow him and, through him, his Father. This relationship is developed through prayer. We meet Jesus in the Scriptures and then bring ourselves deeply into dialogue with him through a rich, connected prayer life.

Meeting him in the depths of our own hearts requires that we live with integrity. Jesus says that anyone who loves him will keep his commandments. If the way we live is out of synch with our beliefs, we will not grow as mature disciples.

Involvement within an ecclesial community

Pope Francis has said, "There is no such thing as a Christian without the Church, a Christian who walks alone, because Jesus inserted himself into the journey of His people" (Homily, May 15, 2014). To be a Christian is to be sent by Jesus "two by two" (Mark 6:7), not to have a solo mission.

We live in an age that emphasizes independence. Many people have a deep thirst for God but believe they can find him better on their own than with a praying community. Many things fuel this thinking, including a heightened individualism and disillusion with the state of many churches.

Still, Jesus made it clear that knowing him and following him requires communal prayer and worship, real fellowship, and collective service to those in need. It is difficult to grow as a Christian disciple without these things.

Charity and justice

Jesus was a Jew, and his teachings are grounded in the faith tradition of Israel that calls people to engage in *tikkun olam*, "repairing the world." Long before Jesus was born, the prophets challenged people to care for the widow, orphan, and stranger, and to bring justice to the land.

Jesus took those teachings further. He said that not only does God favor those who are poor, but in fact God reveals himself in them. He said that God will judge us based on how we have cared for people in need.

We also find in the teachings of Jesus a call to challenge and change the systems that oppress people. We must be people who work for justice.

Forgiveness and mellowness of heart

None of us can move to mature discipleship unless we are willing to set aside our pride and forgive those who offend us. The older son in the parable must come to terms with his anger and move beyond that to the open-heartedness his father embodies.

Some people go through all the motions of being Christians but remain bitter, judgmental, or hard-hearted. St. John of the Cross wrote extensively on how to imitate Christ who shows us how to accept and forgive.

Reading through these four stages of discipleship and the actions they require may make you pause, but Fr. Rolheiser notes, "Jesus doesn't call the ready, he calls the willing!" Think of the apostles and all the others who followed Jesus: Each was human, flawed, and limited; but at the same time, each was willing to keep walking with the Lord.

The Struggles of Mature Discipleship

Mature discipleship is not without its challenges. Here are a few that you might recognize:

Battling the Canaanites

In the Book of Exodus, we read that the people of Israel must slay all the Canaanites in order to claim the Promised Land. Read literally, this story is horrifying. Read metaphorically, the story reveals its meaning, suggests Fr. Rolheiser. We might think of the Canaanites as the old habits and ways of being that keep our souls from advancing to a newer life—the Promised Land, as it were. To be the people we are called to be, we must slay the "Canaanites" within us.

Members of twelve-step fellowships understand this. They have to give up old habits such as drinking, gambling, and internet sexing, and they also have to give up the "people, places and things" that come with those destructive patterns.

Even further, they must take steps to shift their patterns of living, let go of negative attitudes and behavior, and embrace health and prosperity.

Loneliness and deciding to love

When old temptations reassert themselves, we may feel an intense loneliness. It may appear that the honeymoon is over. That relationship we thought would fill the void doesn't do so. We are painfully aware of the flaws of those around us. All that we have built—career, home, family— appears imperfect. Our horizons feel limited.

All of these forces challenge us to grow in spiritual maturity. Love is no longer something that comes to us from the myths and energy of a "honeymoon" experience; rather, it is something that occurs out of our own decisions. We discover that love doesn't just happen to us, but that we must literally decide to love.

Resenting duty and joylessness bordering on anger

Many of us are working very hard to sustain ourselves and our households. Many of us are in that phase of life in which we are responsible for the lives of others, including children and elders. There is no one to whom we can "pass the buck."

How we relate to all of this—just as how we relate to loving—is a choice. We can choose to be resentful, burdened, and joyless, or we can be grateful and joyful. Many people wish late in life that when they were younger and distracted by responsibilities they had been less driven and more appreciative of the richness of their lives. Rarely do they think that they should have worked more.

Workaholism

Because the years of midlife are so demanding, there is a temptation to place work before all other obligations. We feel pressure to achieve and can become slaves to the need to generate income. Or we can lose ourselves in commitments that start with good will but develop into sources of resentment. We may derive our identity and self-worth more from our work than from our close relationships: What we do is more important than who we are. Work becomes as dangerous an escape as is abuse of any substance. But in some ways, workaholism is even more insidious, because its fruit can bring so much approval from society.

Acedia/noonday devil

The desert fathers and mothers, who lived in the barren regions of Egypt in the third through fifth centuries, described the sadness that comes upon us for seemingly no reason as "acedia" or "the noonday devil." This is different from the depression and grief we experience with a loss such as the death of a loved one or the relocation of a friend. In those circumstances, we understandably experience depression and grief.

The "noonday devil" thrusts us into depression and self-absorption when we least expect it. Perhaps an old song triggers it. We hear of someone's good fortune or accomplishment, and rather than feeling joy for that person, we are jealous and feel sorrow for ourselves. In the years in which we are building our lives, we are particularly vulnerable to "acedia."

The struggle to forgive

As we mature, we are called, even forced, to deal with the wounds of our early lives. Fr. Rolheiser asserts that everyone has some experience of a lack of love, affirmation, or being valued as a child. Too many have experiences that were violent or cruel. We find ourselves dealing with anger and bitterness regarding what happened—or did not happen—for us as children. Often this occurs when we are in our thirties.

We find ourselves moving through the hurt and anger. We age, and life brings perspective. We find sources of healing and growth. Without needing to deny our earlier reality, we come to a place of forgiveness and sometimes even acceptance.

In the next session, we will explore the religious faults that can impede mature discipleship. We'll see how some of the stories and parables of Jesus illuminate a way through these obstacles and support us in developing ourselves in the Christian spirituality that characterizes mature discipleship.

✢ ✢ ✢

Sharing Our Faith

✠ This session asked us to examine the four elements that move us from essential discipleship to mature discipleship: Private prayer and private integrity; involvement within an ecclesial community; charity and justice; and forgiveness and mellowness of heart. In which area are you strong? In which area do you need to develop?

✠ Fr. Rolheiser recognizes that living as a mature disciple brings great temptations and challenges. After prayer and reflection, which "Canaanites" are most in the way within you? What would you have to do to let go of them?

✠ Of the forces that most challenge your mature discipleship, which is most prevalent at this moment of your life? How do you experience loneliness and the challenge of deciding to love? The weight of duty or anger? Workaholism? The noonday devil? The struggle to forgive? What are some steps you can take to change this habit or struggle you face?

Living the Good News

Where do you find yourself stirred by the Word of God and his presence among and within your group? What action might you take in response to this? Share with your group what you will do, within the context of your own life, to act upon what you have experienced.

We offer a few examples for you to consider. You can act individually or as a group. If you find that one of these examples touches you, by all means use it, but you may also think of other individual or group actions that inspire you.

Reflect in your journal this week as to where you are in the journey of discipleship. Re-read the introduction and this week's reflection. Make an honest assessment of where you are on the path from essential discipleship to mature discipleship. In prayer, invite God to illuminate your journey.

Movement to mature discipleship is not automatic, says Fr. Rolheiser, and he suggests four areas of practice that support it: Private prayer and integrity, prayer in a church community, works of charity and acts of justice, and forgiveness. Are you taking action in all these areas? Consider partnering with someone in your group who shares your need to grow in a certain area, and do something (such as returning to Mass, incorporating private prayer, being of service to people who are in need, or giving to charity in some way) that will help you develop in that area.

Do you know someone whom you would characterize as a mature disciple? What do you notice about that person? Make time to meet with someone who embodies this phase of discipleship and invite that person to tell you his or her story of faith.

Closing Prayer

Share together prayers of intercession or praise.
Then pray this closing prayer together:

> Good and gracious God,
> You are the source of unimaginable love
> and infinite mercy.
> Open our hearts to your ways
> so that as we progress on this journey,
> we are drawn closer to you
> and one another.
> Send us the grace of your Holy Spirit
> to light our way.
> In the name of Jesus, we pray.
> Amen.

✛ ✛ ✛

Looking Ahead

Prepare for your next session by prayerfully reading and studying
Session 2. You can also supplement your preparation by reading
Sacred Fire *by Ronald Rolheiser, pages 83-95.*

Informal Gathering

The Religious Faults of Mature Adults

The Seven Deadly Sins

Sharing

Briefly share on one of the following questions:

"How am I right now?" or
"What good news would I like to share?"

Sharing the Good News

Share how you did with your action response from the last session (Living the Good News) or how you were able to incorporate the message of the last session into your daily life.

Lifting Our Hearts

... in Song

Play or sing the following song or another song of your choosing:

"Everyday God"

... in the Quiet

Pause for a few moments of silence, and allow yourself to more deeply embrace the presence of God.

... in the Word

Read aloud Luke 6:37-42

As the reader proclaims the sacred text, allow yourself to ponder a word, a phrase, a question, or a feeling that rises up from within you. Reflect on this in silence; when you are invited, briefly share it aloud with our group.

(If no one wishes to speak, simply allow the group to be enveloped in the silence, and allow the reflection to continue for a few more moments.)

... in Prayer

> Loving God,
> we come to you in the midst of busy lives.
> So many concerns and obligations weigh on our minds.
> We run and race from person to person
> from commitment to commitment,
> from place to place,
> barely able to stop and breathe.
> Be with us in this time of connection and stillness,
> this time of slowing and sharing.
> Light a path for us in the insight of this group
> so that we can be more conscious of your will for us
> and aware of your presence among us
> today and every day.
> We pray this in the name of Jesus.
> Amen.

Our Companion on the Journey

Martha and Mary

> Martha her love and joy expressed
> By care to entertain her guest;

While Mary sat to hear her Lord,
And could not bear to lose a word.

The principle in both the same,
Produced in each a different aim;
The one to feast the Lord was led,
The other waited to be fed.

But Mary chose the better part,
Her Saviour's words refreshed her heart;
While busy Martha angry grew,
And lost her time and temper too.

With warmth she to her sister spoke,
But brought upon herself rebuke;
One thing is needful, and but one,
Why do thy thoughts on many run?

How oft are we like Martha vexed,
Encumbered, hurried, and perplexed!
While trifles so engross our thought,
The one thing needful is forgot.

Lord teach us this one thing to choose,
Which they who gain can never lose;
Sufficient in itself alone,
And needful, were the world our own.

Let groveling hearts the world admire,
Thy love is all that I require!
Gladly I may the rest resign,
If the one needful thing be mine!

John Newton

I N THE GOSPELS WE MEET not only Jesus but an entire community of people that embraced him in his earthly life. Fully human as well as fully God, Jesus was surrounded by his family, close friends, and eager acquaintances. Three people were particularly important to him: a brother and two sisters who lived in the town of Bethany outside of Jerusalem—Lazarus, Martha, and Mary.

In one passage we find the sisters hosting a visit by Jesus. Martha is in the kitchen, preparing a meal. Unlike her sister, Mary sits at the Lord's feet, eager to listen and to learn. Martha is irritated that her sister isn't helping. Jesus gently chides her: She should not be irritated; Mary has chosen the better place.

Male or female, all of us know the tug between the "Martha" and "Mary" within us. We may have chosen the person with whom we want to build our personal lives. Perhaps we have added children to our household with all the busyness that entails. Many of us are putting enormous energy into our careers and establishing our professional reputations. We struggle to remain daughters and sons and, at the same time, be "parents" to our aging parents. If we are retired, we may find that life is just as demanding as it was in earlier phases of partnership and parenting. We may find that our "nest" is anything but empty, and our parenting far from over. At best, life is full; at worst, it can be unreasonably busy. Too often, it feels as if there is little to no space for quiet, contemplation, and prayerful personal growth.

Many of us are sympathetic to Martha: "Come

on, be reasonable! There is work to be done! No time for sitting around indulging our 'Mary' urges." As we become mature disciples, however, we realize that the task is not to choose between action and contemplation but to learn how to keep the two practices in balance. We must learn to honor and fulfill the commitments we've made but not become so overtaxed that our interior lives remain barren and neglected. Mary and Martha represent two sides of a spiritual coin. We must learn to honor each face so that in harmony we can create a whole person—a truly mature disciple.

Encountering Wisdom for Life

IN SESSION 1, WE EXAMINED the many struggles that we face as adulthood refines us spiritually. We change and grow as we face and overcome a wide range of personal faults and character defects.

The tradition of the Church describes categories of human propensities that, if acted upon, constitute the seven "deadly" or "capital" sins: pride, lust, anger, greed, envy, gluttony, and sloth. These are called deadly sins especially because they lead to other sins and vices. Each of the deadly sins may challenge us on the road to mature discipleship.

Pride

In this phase of our spiritual growth, pride takes more subtle forms than it does in our youth. We may be making life choices that look self-sacrificing or humble. However, if we look below the surface, we may see that our actions are in reality feeding our self-image. What looks noble on the outside has a shadowy interior. We are motivated more by looking good than by self-lessness.

Fr. Rolheiser is a priest of the Missionary Oblates of Mary. Much of his life has been spent in academic settings, and he also has served twice as the provincial superior of his order's home province. He is known internationally as an author and teacher. In discussing pride, he notes that he has had an urge at times to live in the inner city, among people who are poor, as a witness to his commitment to social justice. On deeper reflection, he's had to admit that while that might look good to friends and colleagues, unless he were willing to completely change his ministry—give up writing and speaking—such a move would be hollow and about his image alone.

We can also become prideful about our prayer lives. We may find ourselves evaluating the spiritual maturity of others and feel a bit smug that we are further along in our development than they are in theirs. Or we may be morbidly focused on the challenges in our prayer lives, which is a sort of pride in reverse. We dwell on our struggles as a way of revealing to others our devoted efforts.

Envy and jealousy

Envy and jealousy can lay claim to us in countless insidious ways as we strive to become mature disciples. Rather than applauding the accomplishments of those that surround us, we find ourselves begrudging their success. We feel threatened by the talents of others. We compare ourselves to others and find them lacking. Our harsh assessments elevate us over others, at least in our own minds. We see examples of this sort of judgment in Martha's envy of Mary and in the parable of the vineyard owner and the workers who wondered why those who arrived late should receive the same wage as those who had worked all day. "Dues paying" becomes the coin of the realm as we fall prey to moralizing and resentment.

Wrath and anger

As mentioned in Session 1, moving toward mature discipleship can bring with it anger about the circumstances and wounds of our early lives. Fr. Rolheiser suggests that the root of the anger we experience in this phase of our development is impatience. Comparing our insides to the outsides of those around us, we lack patience with ourselves, others, and ultimately with God. This can happen with the people we love the most. We make judgments about our spouse, parents, siblings, or children. We judge circumstances to be unfair or even unjust. The wounds we receive as children return to trouble the waters of important relationships.

Selfishness can fuel this anger. We may look at our circumstances, compare them with those of others, and find ourselves bitter. We may be seized with an overwhelming sense of anger that somehow life has not been fair. "Could of," "Should have," and "If only" become our battle cries.

Sloth

For the most part, people are not lazy or lacking in ambition. If anything, most of us are guilty of the behaviors that characterize this age of frenetic striving. So what does sloth look like in

mature disciples? For many, it takes the form of procrastination. We put off what we need to do in our lives. We are challenged by the responsibility of being adults, and so we try to avoid growing and changing. We do not undertake the work we need to do to come to terms with the forces of our sexuality. We are unwilling to deal with our impatience and anger. And we avoid developing our prayer lives or opening our hearts to the people we find challenging.

Sloth can be particularly crafty in how it manifests itself. We may fill our lives with activity, working tremendously hard, as a strategy to hide our emotional and spiritual sloth. Our busyness can be way of avoiding the interior work of true personal growth and change.

Greed

When we think of greed, we think of people like Mr. Potter in Frank Capra's movie *It's a Wonderful Life*—a person who has enormous wealth but who craves even more, even if that means the destruction of a well-meaning small businessman like George Bailey.

In reality, most adults grapple with greed in much subtler forms. "What we want to accumulate is experience, status, and reputation," writes Fr. Rolheiser. We crave being admired even more than we crave social standing and status symbols. Greed places us far from the sort of spiritual humility that characterizes a truly mature disciple. Our greed can take the form of consumerism—the compulsion to follow the latest fad, wear the latest style, or own the latest phone, all of which can have a negative impact on our planet.

Gluttony

In many ways, we live in an age of addiction. It is a rare household that has not been touched by alcoholism, drug abuse, misuse of the internet, gambling, or spending issues. It appears that a significant spiritual challenge of this era is reining in appetites that have run amok.

Sometimes surrender to our appetites takes subtle form or even a form that receives social approval—such as overwork, consumption, and hyper-productivity. Fr. Rolheiser suggests that the huge appetite within each human person has a divine origin; it is part of having the divine life within us. Like God, we long to "drink up the whole world and make love to it." But these good appetites can morph into serious problems.

Lust

Lust is an extreme expression of the natural trait of human desire. Most of us first experience lust in adolescence to early adulthood when the fire of our sexuality is most intense. But even after we may have tamed some of the forces of our sexual desire, our actions can still be lustful. Fr. Rolheiser suggests that the opposite of lust is "purity of heart."

> To be pure of heart is to relate to others and to the world in a way that respects and honors the full dignity, value, and destiny of every person and every being on the planet. To be pure of heart is to see others as God sees them and to love them with their good, not our own, in mind. To be pure of heart is to see others in a way that fully respects their sexuality. Purity of heart is purity of intention.

Many people laughed when President Jimmy Carter admitted, "I've committed adultery in my heart many times." However, his candor was a reflection of his willingness to take seriously the exhortation made by Jesus that even looking at someone with lust is a form of adultery [Matthew 5:28]. Jesus was pointing to the interior work mature discipleship demands. Letting our sexual energy flow in a healthy, life-giving way is part of coming into a deeper maturity.

Examining ourselves and our lives using the lens of the seven deadly sins need not be a depressing or upsetting task. Making an honest assessment of ourselves can launch us into a new chapter of selflessness and service. To become a mature disciple is to be willing to be more self-aware and self-giving—and that requires interior work. In the decades of adulthood, we can become better, more generous, and more contributing people in our families, our communities, and the world at large.

✠ ✠ ✠

Sharing Our Faith

✠ Are you a Mary or a Martha? Or are you both? In what way do you resemble either or both of the sisters? How balanced is your life?

✠ What was your reaction to the discussion of the seven deadly sins in this session? Did you find it easy to move from a superficial reading of pride, envy, wrath, sloth, greed, gluttony, and lust to the deeper, more nuanced meaning Fr. Rolheiser offers? How do you identify these qualities within yourself?

✠ What would "purity of heart" look like in your life?

Living the Good News

Where do you find yourself stirred by the Word of God and his presence among and within your group? What action might you take in response to this? Share with your group what you will do, within the context of your own life, to act upon what you have experienced.

We offer a few examples for you to consider here. These are just examples. You can act individually or as a group. If you find that one of these examples touches you, by all means use it, but you may also think of other individual or group actions that inspire you.

Make a date with a group member or friend to discuss how each of you balances his or her life between meeting obligations and spending time with God.

Gluttony is not limited to eating and drinking; it can be part anything we consume to excess. Why do you think appetite in all its forms is so dominant a challenge today? How are appetite and addiction related? As a group, visit an "open" twelve-step meeting in your town. Afterward, discuss why addiction requires a spiritual as well as emotional and physical solution.

Give some of your time to an organization that is about supporting the dignity of other people or other creatures. This could be serving in a soup kitchen; participating in a parish service project such as Habitat for Humanity; joining with friends and family to clean a park or roadside; or joining one of the many organizations that support clean water, conservation or protection of wildlife, and safety and quality in agriculture and food processing.

✛ ✛ ✛

Closing Prayer

Share together prayers of intercession or praise.

Then pray this closing prayer together:

> Jesus,
> we thank you for this time together.
> We thank you for the wisdom you offered us
> as we reflected on our lives and experience.
> Help us in the days ahead to be
> the active source of your hospitality

in the manner of your dear friend Martha.
Help us remember that we cannot serve you
    unless we make time
to sit at your feet like your dear friend Mary.
Let your spirit animate us in all that we do.
Amen.

Looking Ahead

Prepare for your next session by prayerfully reading and studying Session 3. You can also supplement your preparation by reading Sacred Fire, *pages 96-104.*

Informal Gathering

Jesus Challenges Us to a More Generous Discipleship

To Look for Christ on the Road to Emmaus

Sharing

Briefly share on one of the following questions:

"How am I right now?" or
"What good news would I like to share?"

Sharing the Good News

Share how you did with your action response from the last session (Living the Good News) or how you were able to incorporate the message of the last session into your daily life.

Lifting Our Hearts ...

... in Song

Play or sing the following song or another song of your choosing:

"For Living, for Dying"

... in the Quiet

Pause for a few moments of silence and allow yourself to more deeply embrace the presence of God.

... in the Word

Read aloud Luke 24:13-35

As the reader proclaims the sacred text, allow yourself to ponder a word, a phrase, a question, or a feeling that rises up from within you. Reflect on this in silence; when you are invited, briefly share it aloud with our group.

(If no one wishes to speak, simply allow the group to be enveloped in the silence, and allow the reflection to continue for a few more moments.)

... in Prayer

Conclude with this prayer spoken together:

> Lord,
> we met you on the road,
> and we were so weary and defeated,
> we failed to see you.
> We spoke with you,
> sharing our crushed hopes and dreams,
> but we resisted your answer.
> We were fleeing bad circumstances,
> and we were too downtrodden to remember all you
>   taught us.
> But when you came to us in the breaking of the bread,
> we saw you again:
> Food for the journey,
> hope for the despairing,
> love for the lost,
> the promise of God fulfilled among us.
> Open our eyes, Lord,
> that we may see you
> wherever we go
> and in a special way in the banquet you give us,
>   the Eucharist.
> In the name of Jesus, we pray.
> Amen.

Our Companion on the Journey

St. Peter

"You are Peter, and upon this rock I will build my church."

Matthew 16:18

"Brothers and sisters, what happened in a unique way in
St. Peter, also takes place in every Christian who develops
a sincere faith in Jesus the Christ, the Son of the living
God. Today's Gospel challenges each of us: How is your
faith? Let each of us answer in our heart. How is your
faith? How is it? What does the Lord find in our hearts:
a firm heart, like a rock? Or a heart like sand, that is,
doubtful, mistrustful, unbelieving? It would do us good to
think about this throughout the day.
If the Lord finds in our hearts a faith—I won't say perfect, but sincere, genuine, then he will see in us, too, the
living rocks on which he builds His community."

Pope Francis, Angelus address, August 24, 2014

MOST OF US HAVE KNOWN someone of deep faith.
Perhaps it was a grandparent or parent, or a
person in ordained or religious life. In our assessment, this person seemed solid in his or her
ability to follow Christ. Comparing our turbulent
"insides" to such a person's "outsides" may have
inspired us. But it may have intimidated us, too.
By comparison, we may have found ourselves
lacking and filled with feelings of inadequacy.
Simon Peter was one of the first disciples Jesus
called to his side. Simon is an ordinary guy, a

fisherman toiling to care for his family. When we meet him in the Gospels, he is working alongside his brother Andrew in the Sea of Galilee outside their village of Capernaum. We are told that upon meeting Jesus, they dropped their nets. Leaving life and livelihood aside, they set off with the Lord.

At first, Peter seems to have an exceptional faith, but as we get to know him, we see both his virtues and his flaws. He is grandiose; it is Peter's idea to build tents for Jesus, Moses, and Elijah after the vision on the mountaintop. Peter is rash and angry; it is he who slices off the ear of Malchus, the high priest's slave, when Jesus is arrested. It is also Peter who, in his devastation and fear, denies the Lord. On the other hand, Peter is insightful and observant: He is the first person to call Jesus the Messiah (Mark 8:29, Luke 9:20, Matthew 16:16-17). He is the first man to run to the empty tomb, believing the account of the women (Luke 24:12). Ultimately, Peter is the rock upon whom Jesus builds his church (Matthew 16:18). Peter proves profoundly faithful and courageous, surmounting his human failings to not only lead the Jerusalem community after the resurrection but to go to his death on a cross as Jesus did.

We may find that there are times that we, like Peter, are flailing about in the area of faith and discipleship. We may seem to have lost our moorings and feel as if we are getting it all wrong.

To embrace a mature discipleship is to be faithful to the task of being alongside Jesus in intimate trust and faithful friendship, no matter how our circumstances appear or what our harsh self-assessments tell us.

Encountering Wisdom for Life

W HEN WE HEAR THE PHRASE "human development," our minds most likely fly to the earliest chapters of life. We think of infancy, childhood, adolescence, and the teen years. In fact, the longest-running chapter of human development is adulthood. These decades are filled with change and challenge, shifts that are often fueled by crisis. The experiences of adulthood can leave us frozen in our emotional tracks or willing to move to new depths of development. These challenges, Fr. Rolheiser writes, "enter our lives not just as challenges to us to retain our balance and stability but, especially, as invitations to stretch our hearts and minds into deeper understanding, deeper compassion, deeper generosity, and deeper maturity."

Fr. Rolheiser writes that there are six invitations in the Gospels that summon us, in times of crisis, to embrace mature discipleship. The first is "to look for Christ on the Road to Emmaus."

The disciples are returning home, devastated by the death of Jesus. Their hopes are dashed; the triumphant entry into Jerusalem that we now commemorate on Palm Sunday was followed by the vicious, shameful, and bloody end to Jesus' earthly life. The promise of the Messiah now seems false, and their faith has been shattered. Even though there have been reports of resurrection, the two head home, crestfallen.

To illuminate the significance of the story in our age, Fr. Rolheiser turns to Dutch theologian Fr. Edward Schillebeeckx, OP. Once, during a lecture, Fr. Schillebeeckx was asked which of the many gospel stories best illustrates the challenge of faith in this era. He replied that it is the story in the Gospel of Luke about the disciples on the road to Emmaus.

Fr. Schillebeeckx observed that in many ways the story of Cleopas and his companion (scholars speculate that they are a husband and wife) parallels the situation of contemporary disciples. The mysteries of faith often are in collision with the dominant secular culture.

In exploring the story, Fr. Rolheiser points out that to walk toward Emmaus and away from Jerusalem is to "walk away from their faith dream, away from the Church, and away from the place where Christ has been humiliated," and toward consolation. We, like the weary duo, may find ourselves at some point in our discipleship throwing our hands in the air, turning our backs, and, like upset teens, muttering "whatever." We want immediate comfort, not challenge. We want to be faithful, but too often feel as if we are sitting somewhere between the dark events of Good Friday and a yet-to-be experienced Easter Sunday.

The two disciples are lucky. They meet Christ on the road, although they do not recognize him. In fact, they are almost scoffing as they accuse him of being the only person who hasn't heard about the events that have transpired in Jerusalem. Jesus, reacting to their deep resignation and discouragement, speaks.

He recounts the sacred story of the Jews, and in the telling he demonstrates that the story of Jesus is an integral part of the plan of God. The crucifixion is not God's plan derailed; it is God's plan made real. Fr. Rolheiser describes the conversation as a "restructuring of imagination." Like people who need corrective lenses to see clearly, Cleopas and his companion must shift their horizon from the surface of their experience and unlock the reality beneath it—a reality that literally stands before them. This happens at the moment of the breaking of the bread—the Eucharist—when they recognize that the Lord is risen and is with them.

In the course of our discipleship, we too will face moments when our faith and hope feel shattered. In the depth of a crisis, a loss, or disillusionment we may be inclined to abandon our faith. In those moments, we forget that the fundamental pattern of the Christian life is the movement from life through death to resurrection. "The humiliation of the cross is the deep secret that not only unlocks a proper understanding of Christ but also unlocks the depth of human wisdom," writes Fr. Rolheiser.

If we are able to stop in the midst of the maelstrom of loss of certainty, we may find that our imaginations—particularly as they engage notions of our faith, our Church, and our God—are being restructured. We may find that as the despair clouding our vision is cast aside, we are able to recognize Christ in altogether new ways. But if we remain locked into seeing God, Christ, and Church in only one way, we may never move beyond despair.

Like the two on the road, when we are looking through the eyes of defeat and cynicism, we will not be able to see Christ. When we reach deep within and look at circumstances through the eyes of a reimagined faith, we will be able to see Christ present and at work. To make this leap is an act of mature faith and mature discipleship.

✛ ✛ ✛

Sharing Our Faith

✛ The two on the road to Emmaus are archetypes for all followers of Jesus. Have you experienced a time when your
faith life felt bereft? The mystics suggest that this is not a crisis of faith but rather a crisis of imagination; it is an inability
to look in a new and deeper way at circumstances, with eyes
that are willing to see God at work. Recall a time when it
was difficult for you to see God's presence in the world, and
share how your perceptions changed.

✛ Why is the story of Emmaus particularly relevant at this time
in human history? Fr. Rolheiser asserts that "the situation of
today's Christians in our secularized cultures is basically the
same: we are walking on the road to Emmaus, discouraged,
our youthful faith crucified, talking with Christ, but unable
to recognize him." How do you handle feelings of discouragement with the culture we live in? With the Church itself?

✛ In this era, when the Church has revealed abuse, and fiscal mismanagement, many Catholics are hurt, angry, and
alienated. How do you continue to be a faithful member of
the Church despite the various scandals? What do you say
to others who are alienated or upset? How is the story of the
Road to Emmaus relevant to these efforts?

Living the Good News

*Where do you find yourself stirred by the Word of God and his pres-
ence among and within your group? What action might you take in
response to this? Share with your group what you will do, within
the context of your own life, to act upon what you have experienced.*

*We offer a few examples for you to consider here. These are just
examples. You can act individually or as a group. If you find that*

one of them touches you, by all means use it, but you may also think
of other individual or group actions that inspire you.

1. The Apostle Peter is a very human follower of Jesus. As his moods swing, his actions follow. Which of the stories about Peter resonates with you in terms of your life experience? In your journal, write about your answer. Share your thoughts with a member of your group or with a friend.

Our discipleship is not lived apart from the Lord. We have been promised that we will see him. This happens profoundly in the Eucharist, when we meet him in the breaking of the bread. It also happens, he tells us, in the hungry, the thirsty, the stranger, the naked, the sick, and the prisoner (Matthew 25:41-43). Select a way to take action and place yourself in service to people facing such duress.

St. Peter is a pivotal leader in the growth of the early Church. Get to know him better by reading the Acts of the Apostles this week. If you live in a family setting, perhaps you can read a short section after a family meal and share its meaning for you.

✠ ✠ ✠

Closing Prayer

Share together prayers of intercession or praise.

Then pray this closing prayer together:

> Ever-forgiving God,
> we thank you for your constant love
> and the embrace that awaits us

every time we return home to you.
Strengthen us in faith
and help us to grow in love,
so that when people meet us,
they also meet you.
Help us ground our service in the convictions
   of our faith
so that when we meet others in their need,
we recognize you.
In the name of Jesus, we pray.
Amen.

Looking Ahead

Prepare for your next session by prayerfully reading and studying Session 4. You can also supplement your preparation by reading Sacred Fire, *pages 104-108.*

Informal Gathering

Fidelity

To Remain Faithful
When We Want to Walk Away

Sharing

Briefly share on one of the following questions:

"How am I right now?" or
"What good news would I like to share?"

Sharing the Good News

Share how you did with your action response from the last session (Living the Good News) or how you were able to incorporate the message of the last session into your daily life.

Lifting Our Hearts

... in Song

Play or sing the following song or another song of your choosing:

"Heal Me, Lord"

... in the Quiet

Pause for a few moments of silence and allow yourself to more deeply embrace the presence of God.

... in the Word

Read aloud John 6:35-69

As the reader proclaims the sacred text, allow yourself to ponder a word, a phrase, a question, or a feeling that rises up from within you. Reflect on this in silence; when you are invited, briefly share it aloud with our group.

(If no one wishes to speak, simply allow the group to be enveloped in the silence, and allow the reflection to continue for a few more moments.)

... in Prayer

Conclude with this prayer spoken together:

> Lord,
> you said to us,
> "I am the bread of life.
> Whoever comes to me will never be hungry,
> and whoever believes in me will never be thirsty."
> We are hungry Lord,
> We are thirsty.
> Forgive us for the times
> we've tried to fill ourselves with food
> that could not satisfy our hunger,
> with drink that could not quench our thirst.
> Open us to receive the fullness of the spiritual drink
>   you offer,
> the bread that sustains us in good times and in bad.
> Make us thankful for all that you have given us.
> May we be as generous as you are
> as we work to serve the needs of others.
> In your holy name we pray, O Christ.
> Amen.

SESSION 4

Our Companion on the Journey

Dietrich Bonhoeffer

"Jesus Christ lived in the midst of his enemies. At the
end all his disciples deserted him. On the Cross he was
utterly alone, surrounded by evildoers and mockers. For
this cause he had come, to bring peace to the enemies of
God. So the Christian, too, belongs not in the seclusion of
a cloistered life but in the thick of foes."

Dietrich Bonhoeffer

DIETRICH BONHOEFFER WAS A German theologian
and Lutheran pastor who was martyred for
participating in an unsuccessful plot to assassinate
Adolf Hitler. A founder of a resistance movement
called the Confessing Church, Dietrich struggled to
reconcile his deep commitment to Christian pacifism and the need to take action in response to the
atrocities being committed by the Nazi regime.

Dietrich's early life was one of privilege and
wealth. His family was moral but not overly religious. A precocious student, he completed more
than one doctoral degree by the age of twenty-
five. Too young to be ordained, he traveled to New
York's Union Theological Seminary.

Frank Fisher, an African-American fellow semi-
narian, invited Bonhoeffer to join him in attending Harlem's Abyssinian Baptist Church. It became
Bonhoeffer's place of worship and service (he
taught Sunday school). Inspired by Pastor Adam
Clayton Powell Sr., Bonhoeffer began reflecting
on the issue of social justice, and particularly the

51

church's inability—or unwillingness—to bring about integration and other forms of social change. He found himself shifting from an intellectual understanding of Christianity to a heartfelt belief in the reality of the love of God.

Bonhoeffer returned to Germany and a teaching position in 1931, and was ordained later that year. His first radio address attacking Hitler occurred two days after the latter was installed as chancellor. Despite their efforts to stop the appointments, Bonhoeffer and his associates saw a majority of church leadership positions filled with Nazi sympathizers. To be faithful required facing his deep inner turmoil with intellectual and spiritual honesty.

Bonhoeffer was arrested in 1943 for his involvement with the German resistance and connections to the failed assassination plot. He was hanged in 1945, one week before the allies reached the camp in which he was being held.

Bonhoeffer exemplifies the willingness to follow Christ at any cost, and to speak Christ's truth even to the point of death.

Encountering Wisdom for Life

OFTEN, WHEN WE UNDERTAKE a new endeavor, we are filled with excitement. The new year comes, and we're ready to take on improving our diet or fitness. The corporate fiscal year turns, and we're ready to achieve new levels of success in our business. Our wedding anniversary arrives, and we resolve to do better about making time for our spouse and nurturing our marriage. The school year kicks off, and we intend to make it more organized and productive.

SESSION 4

Over time, our zeal begins to wane. Tasks that were novel become mundane. We find ourselves questioning our commitment; things just don't seem as rosy as they did at the start. It's getting hard to remain committed to the goals we have set.

In the same way, we can find ourselves losing heart as disciples. Staying faithful sometimes feels hard. At this point, the challenge to mature discipleship is overcoming disillusionment. "The challenge then will be to act out of value rather than out of feeling and to act out of trust rather than out of understanding," explains Fr. Rolheiser. He offers the Apostle Peter, as depicted in the Gospel of John, as an example of someone who, in the face of deep disillusionment and questioning, remains faithful.

The story of note appears in John's Gospel in what is called the "bread of life discourse." Jesus uses language that would be, for his time, extremely jarring. He says to his followers, "Unless you eat the flesh of the Son of Man and drink his blood, you can have no life in you" (John 6:53). This would have been shocking to those listening to him; many would have thought that he was referring to cannibalism. John notes that some of those following Jesus stopped following him upon hearing this directive.

Jesus challenges his followers. Peter responds, "Lord, to whom shall we go? You have the words of everlasting life." This is a stunning response. Although he doesn't entirely understand Jesus (as revealed in many other stories about Peter), and although he may have been shocked by the Lord's language, he remains committed. Peter's answer, Fr. Rolheiser writes, is the "paradigm for mature and sustained commitment." Even though remaining true to Jesus may mean death, Peter is willing to stand alongside him. Peter chooses fidelity to his relationship with Jesus.

Anyone who has been in a long-term committed relationship such as a marriage, religious vocation, or a life-long friendship, understands that sometimes the only thing that sustains the connection to someone important is simple fidelity. Walking away may be attractive, but it is not an option. Bound by a promise to be there for each other, the partners in a commitment honor the ties that bind.

C.S. Lewis provides an example as he describes his adult conversion to Christianity not as a moment of peak experience but as an act of confused, reluctant desperation. He describes himself, as he knelt down to pray, "as the most dejected and reluctant convert in all England." But although resistant, he embraced Jesus Christ, because he knew that the hardness of God is kinder than the softness of human beings "and His compulsion is our liberation."

What exactly is "God's compulsion?" Fr. Rolheiser describes it as a deep, internal sense that exceeds mere thought or feeling. It is the intuitive knowing of the action we must take to live authentically. "God's compulsion" is a call to a faithfulness not based on our feelings, but based on our commitment.

The phase of mature discipleship can be lengthy. We may find ourselves, at times, bored and eager for a change. Perhaps we long for the arrival of a "second honeymoon" that doesn't come. When Mother Teresa died, letters she had written to her spiritual directors were given to the priest assigned to prepare for her beatification. Many were surprised to hear that she felt an "interior darkness" for many years and that she often felt unloved by God. In 1959 she wrote, "In my soul, I feel just the terrible pain of loss, of God not wanting me, of God not being God, of God not really existing." But despite an interior life that often felt barren, she continued her work among Calcutta's poorest people. She acted out of faith, not feeling.

Although some found the content of her letters shocking, others were deeply inspired by them. Although struggling with a feeling of being distant from God, they realized staying faithful was in fact an act of holiness—as it had been for Mother Teresa.

Fr. Rolheiser recognizes that not all major moments of disillusionment should be dismissed. Some require thought and discernment. Mother Teresa did not go it alone; she had friends and advisers who helped her discern the path of following Jesus. Fr. Rolheiser suggests that the central question—what do you really want to do here—can be considered on three levels:

- What do I think is *the wisest thing to do* here?
- What would *I most like to do* here?
- What do *I have to do* here?

Dietrich Bonhoeffer struggled with the challenge of doing right. He agonized over the actions that he and other members of the German resistance were contemplating in opposition to Hitler. He did not act out of whim or in a cavalier manner, but sought to discover how the light of the Gospel illuminated the world around him. In his book *Ethics*, he writes:

> Do and dare what is right, not swayed by the whim of the moment. Bravely take hold of the real, not dallying now with what might be. Not in the flight of ideas but only in action is freedom. Make up your mind and come out into the tempest of living. God's command is enough and your faith in him to sustain you. Then at last freedom will welcome your spirit amid great rejoicing.

Sharing Our Faith

✠ There are many things to be faithful to in our daily lives. Have you ever had an experience of struggling with fidelity? What was it? What things supported you in being faithful? What undermined your faithfulness? What lessons did you take from your experience?

✠ Do you have a companion who supports you in your spiritual development? How is this person helpful?

✠ Fr. Rolheiser offers a simple three-level inventory: What do I think is the wisest thing to do here? What would I most like to do here? What do I have to do here? Is there a situation in your life in which you can apply this tool? Explain.

Living the Good News

Where do you find yourself stirred by the Word of God and his presence among and within your group? What action might you take in response to this? Share with your group what you will do, within the context of your own life, to act upon what you have experienced.

We offer a few examples for you to consider here. These are just examples. You can act individually or as a group. If you find that one of them touches you, by all means use it, but you may also think of other individual or group actions that inspire you.

🌐 Rent the movie *Bonhoeffer* and watch it with group mates, friends, or family. What quality did the Rev. Dr. Bonhoeffer's faith have? In what ways are you like him? In what ways does his martyrdom challenge you to grow?

🌐 Bill Wilson, the founder of the international movement Alcoholics Anonymous said: "You can't think your way into right action, but you can act your way into right thinking." What actions can you take this week to deepen your faithfulness?

 Is there a situation in your life in which it is easier to stay silent than to speak? What forces keep contemporary Christians from speaking up? As you go through life this week, see if there is a setting in which sharing the perspective of your faith would be helpful.

✠ ✠ ✠

Closing Prayer

Share together prayers of intercession or praise.

Then pray this closing prayer together:

> Loving God,
> You meet us in the wonders of our lives
> and also in the trials.
> You come to us in the refreshing rain of spring,
> and the freezing wind of winter.
> Help us to trust that there is grace unfolding
> when our spiritual lives seem dead or barren.
> Help us to become more faithful to you
> and more willing to bear witness to your love and
>   mercy.
> We know that you are present
> no matter how we feel.
> We trust in you, Jesus, and pray this prayer in your
>   name.
> Amen.

Looking Ahead

Prepare for your next session by prayerfully reading and studying Session 5. You can also supplement your preparation by reading Sacred Fire, *pages 109 to 115.*

Informal Gathering

Torn Loyalties

To Walk as Both "Son of David" and as "Lord" Inside the Regions of Tyre and Sidon

Sharing

Briefly share on one of the following questions:

"How am I right now?" or
"What good news would I like to share?"

Sharing the Good News

Share how you did with your action response from the last session (Living the Good News) or how you were able to incorporate the message of the last session into your daily life.

Lifting Our Hearts

... in Song

Play or sing the following song or another song of your choosing:

"Gathered in the Love of Christ"

... in the Quiet

Pause for a few moments of silence, and allow yourself to more deeply embrace the presence of God.

... in the Word

Read aloud Mark 7:24-30

As the reader proclaims the sacred text, allow yourself to ponder a word, a phrase, a question, or a feeling that rises up from within you. Reflect on this in silence; when you are invited, briefly share it aloud with the group.

(If no one wishes to speak, simply allow the group to be enveloped in the silence, and allow the reflection to continue for a few more moments.)

... in Prayer

> Jesus,
> your companions in earthly life
> recognized you as the long-awaited
> Messiah of your people, Israel.
> Only as time passed
> did they understand that you were a gift
> given to the entire human family.
> Help us know you and proclaim you
> as the universal God,
> the one who comes to establish
> the reign of justice and love
> for all people in all places,
> in every age and time.
> Amen.

Our Companion on the Journey

St. Teresa Benedicta of the Cross (Edith Stein)

"The unbounded loving surrender to God and God's return gift, full and enduring union, this is the highest elevation of the heart attainable for the highest level of prayer. Souls who have attained it are truly the heart of the church and in them lives Jesus' high priestly love... For those blessed souls who have entered into the unity of life in God, everything is one: rest and activity, looking and acting, silence and speaking, listening and communicating, surrender in loving acceptance and an outpouring of love in grateful songs of praise."

St. Teresa Benedicta

ST. TERESA BENEDICTA OF THE CROSS (born Edith Stein) was a Carmelite sister, philosopher, and mystic who was martyred in the Nazi death camp at Auschwitz in 1942 and canonized by Pope St. John Paul II in 1998. She was youngest of eleven children in a devout Jewish family in Breslau, Germany (now Wroclaw, Poland). Although her family practiced their faith, her later writings reveal that she was an atheist by her teens and twenties.

Edith was a brilliant scholar, and her studies led to her interest in Christianity. She spent an entire night reading an autobiography of St. Teresa of Ávila and later wrote, "When I had finished that book, I said to myself: This is the truth."

Edith was baptized into the Catholic Church in 1922 and began teaching at a Dominican sisters' school. She joined the Carmelites of Cologne in 1934 and made final vows in 1938. While there, she was given permission to write a book focusing on the life of a Jewish family. It was her desire to witness to the beauty of Judaism in opposition to the escalating Nazi terrorism.

Sr. Teresa Benedicta wrote to Pope Pius XI in 1933 to implore him to act on behalf of the Jews:

> Everything that happened and continues to happen on a daily basis originates with a government that calls itself "Christian." For weeks not only Jews but also thousands of faithful Catholics in Germany, and, I believe, all over the world, have been waiting and hoping for the Church of Christ to raise its voice to put a stop to this abuse of Christ's name.

She received no reply from the pope, who at the time was trying to reach an accommodation with the German government. In 1937, the disillusioned pope issued an encyclical, which was smuggled into Germany and read in every Catholic Church, condemning the abuses of the Nazi regime. That encyclical resulted in intensified persecution of the Church and of Catholics.

Because she was Jewish, Sr. Teresa Benedicta was in grave danger as Nazi violence in Cologne intensified. Her religious community smuggled her and her sister Rosa, also a Carmelite, to Holland. However, when the Catholic bishops of Holland issued a pastoral letter decrying the persecution and deportation of the Jews, the Nazis retaliated by rounding up all Dutch Jews and people with Jewish origins.

Rosa and Sr. Theresa Benedicta were arrested at the convent in 1942 and transported by train to Auschwitz. They, as well as all the others on their transport, were gassed immediately upon arrival. Sr. Theresa Benedicta was 51.

Encountering Wisdom for Life

TO BE A HUMAN BEING is to be on an ever evolving journey of belonging. For Christians, the sacrament of baptism is the profound gesture that proclaims our place within the community of believers. In the rite, the priest declares "I claim you for Christ." Anointed with the holy oil and submerged in the waters of life, we become one with the Christian family.

The path to adulthood brings with it other forms of belonging. We belong to classroom groups, sports teams. We identify ourselves with our high school and college communities and adopt their nicknames—we're Eagles, or Hoyas, or Knights. We claim our work communities as sources of identity, and we certainly find a sense of belonging in the church circles of which we are a part.

As we grow as part of a family, group, or religious circle, we change. As we do, we may find that once-taken-for-granted affinities do not seem as strong. We may notice that we are no longer as like-minded with the group as we once were. Facing the gap, we may find our loyalties are stretched and our certainty shaken.

This process is a natural part of growing in depth as followers of Christ. To become a mature disciple is to risk finding ourselves stretched to the point of breaking. Fr. Rolheiser suggests that we, like Jesus, have to embrace "feeling torn between being a loyal child of our faith tradition and being a universal instrument of salvation for our God." The gospel story (Mark 7:24-30) he offers us to illuminate this reality is that of the interaction between Jesus and the Syrophoenician woman (In Matthew's Gospel, 15:21-28, the woman is described as Canaanite).

The early Christians would have understood the drama inherent in this story. Jesus is not among his own people; he is in pagan territory in the region of Tyre. The woman who approaches him is Greek, a descendant of the Canaanites— the bitter enemies of the Jews who were driven out of their territory at God's command. Despite her gender and her foreign roots, she approaches Jesus in faith, desperate for help.

This story is not only about a miracle, it is also about a controversy: How dare she ask anything of the Messiah who has been sent to the Jews? Her language reveals awareness that she is transgressing boundaries: She addresses Jesus as "Son of David." His response is to insult her, to, in effect, call her a dog. While this may shock us, it would not have shocked his friends, who would have agreed with him about her lack of status.

Despite the insult, she does not relent. In total humility, she accepts his insult and continues her appeal, this time addressing him only as "Lord" and reminding him that even the dogs are fed. Jesus, in turn, responds with like humility and wisdom and rethinks his response. He extols her faith and tells her that her child is cured.

Fr. Rolheiser points out that in many ways our churches are in the same position as was Jesus. We are, in so many ways, on new turf. We are ministering in a time of great cultural and religious plurality. Old loyalties from a time of black-and-white certitude are being challenged. Fr. Rolheiser suggests that in this story Jesus is torn between his identity as Messiah for the Jews (Son of David) and his identity as God for all (Lord).

That pull—between loyalty to the sense of identity provided by a great faith tradition and a willingness to expand the boundaries of that tradition—is experienced in the Catholic Church today. The terms of politics are generally used to describe the polarity: As a "conservative," notes Fr. Rolheiser, each believer is responsible for seeking out the lost sheep of his or her religious tradition. As a progressive, each believer is called to think beyond the boundaries of religious particularity and "be a universal instrument of salvation to all the world."

This is, to put it mildly, a profound tension. "One part of us is called to minister to our own, and that brings with it its own set of rules; another part of us is called to minister to the whole world, and some of the house rules no longer apply then," he says.

To illuminate the quandary, Fr. Rolheiser tells of a pastoral dilemma he once faced. Rather than giving him an easy answer, his bishop pointed out to him all the threads that he could consider in formulating a decision, including the mind of the Church, Canon Law, the realities of the particular parish community involved, diocesan regulations, the pastoral need of the people, and more. In Roman Catholicism, this is called subsidiarity, allowing a decision to be made by those in authority at the most local level possible. The bishop trusted Fr. Rolheiser to integrate both identities he claimed as an ordained pastoral leader—the characteristics of "Son of David" and "Lord" embodied by Jesus—and make the right decision.

It is simpler to choose either/or but the mature disciple is able to stand in the tension of these two polarities. The mature disciple is able to journey in prayer and community to a "both/and" perspective as exemplified in the way Jesus finally responds to the Syrophoenician woman.

✠ ✠ ✠

Sharing Our Faith

✠ What do you make of the bold and faithful Syrophoenician woman? In what ways is she ministering to Jesus himself in this story? In what ways is she an example of deep faith?

✠ What do you make of the tension between the requirements of church programs (for example, the conditions set for receiving sacraments such as matrimony, baptism, and Eucharist) and the call to be "a universal instrument of salvation for everyone?"

✠ How do you relate to the rules of your faith tradition? How do you respond to people who do not relate to the rules in the same way?

Living the Good News

Where do you find yourself stirred by the Word of God and his presence among and within your group? What action might you take in response to this? Share with your group what you will do, within the context of your own life, to act upon what you have experienced.

We offer a few examples for you to consider here. These are just examples. You can act individually or as a group. If you find that one of them touches you, by all means use it, but you may also think of other individual or group actions that inspire you.

🌐 In your journal, write about your loyalties and about areas in which you experience "torn loyalties." Pray for open-mindedness and tolerance of people with perspectives different from your own.

🌐 Seek out someone you know who relates differently than you do to the Roman Catholic tradition. Have a conversation with this person, but try to do more listening than questioning. Despite your differences, what values of yours does this person uphold?

As a group, visit a parish with a worship style that differs significantly from your own or a church of another faith tradition. Afterwards, share your observations with each other, but do so in a noncritical, affirmative way. See if you can identify and hold the tension of being loyal to your way of doing things and accepting that the Christian faith transcends style or preference.

✦ ✦ ✦

Closing Prayer

Share together prayers of intercession or praise.

Then pray this closing prayer together:

> O God who came
> as Son of David and Lord of all,
> help us to see the countless ways
> your people express
> authentic belief in you.
> Open our hearts to receive the wisdom held
> by brothers and sisters
> whose point of view
> differs from our own.
> Give us expansive eyes
> that see beyond boundaries—
> eyes like those of your faithful daughter,
> Sr. Teresa Benedicta of the Cross.
> In the name of Jesus, we pray.
> Amen.

Looking Ahead

Prepare for your next session by prayerfully reading and studying Session 6. You can also supplement your preparation by reading Sacred Fire, *pages 115 to 127.*

Informal Gathering

SESSION 6

Compassion and Mercy

To Be Perfect as Our Heavenly Father is Perfect

Sharing

Briefly share on one of the following questions:

"How am I right now?" or
"What good news would I like to share?"

Sharing the Good News

Share how you did with your action response from the last session (Living the Good News) or how you were able to incorporate the message of the last session into your daily life.

Lifting Our Hearts

... in Song

Play or sing the following song or another song of your choosing:

"Anthem: We Are Called, We Are Chosen"

... in the Quiet

Pause for a few moments of silence and allow yourself to more deeply embrace the presence of God.

... in the Word

Read aloud Luke 15:1-10

As the reader proclaims the sacred text, allow yourself to ponder a word, a phrase, a question, or a feeling that rises up from within you. Reflect on this in silence; when you are invited, briefly share it aloud with our group.

(If no one wishes to speak, simply allow the group to be enveloped in the silence, and allow the reflection to continue for a few more moments.)

... in Prayer

> Loving God,
> from age to age you gather
> your people into your arms.
> No one stands outside your expansive
>   and loving grasp.
> Help us to see you in each other
> and to hear your voice,
> particularly when we feel resistant or defiant,
> righteous or judgmental.
> Be with us, Lord, as we open ourselves to each other
>   in this circle.
> Help us meet each other in the same spirit
> of acceptance, love, and service
> you demonstrated when you took towel and basin
> and gently bathed the feet of the disciples.
> In the name of Jesus, we pray.
> Amen.

Our Companion on the Journey

Henri Nouwen

"Through compassion it is possible to recognize that the craving for love that [people] feel resides also in our own hearts, that the cruelty the world knows all too well is also rooted in our own impulses. Through compassion we also sense our hope for forgiveness in our friends' eyes and our hatred in their bitter mouths. When they kill, we know that we could have done it; when they give life, we know that we can do the same. For a compassionate person nothing human is alien: no joy and no sorrow, no way of living and no way of dying."

Henri J.M. Nouwen, *The Wounded Healer*

HENRI NOUWEN WAS A DUTCH-BORN Catholic priest whose writing on spiritual subjects—he wrote 39 books in all—influenced millions worldwide. He taught in a number of prestigious settings, but he is best known for his work as a spiritual seeker and guide, particularly as shaped and developed through his friendship with Jean Vanier, the founder of the global network of L'Arche communities. The L'Arche network, founded in 1964 on the belief that meaningful activity is central to human dignity, allows people with intellectual disabilities to live alongside normally abled people who assist them.

In the L'Arche movement, Henri Nouwen saw the principles about which he preached and taught put into practice every day. Although Nouwen had spent his life as a priest, monk, psychologist, academic, and missionary, he had not seen Christian community lived as powerfully in other set-tings. At L'Arche, people who might otherwise be rejected were recognized as having prophetic gifts to share. In his later years, Nouwen often brought members of his L'Arche community on his travels. Their presence in his life opened up new horizons of compassion and love.

Nouwen's struggles with depression, loneliness, and community led him to write emotionally and spiritually intimate books unfolding the themes of compassion, solitude, love, and forgiveness. His warmth and candor made clear that he was not an expert imparting directions but a fellow traveler, a wounded healer willing to share the insights he gained through his often challenging personal journey.

Encountering Wisdom for Life

EVERY GARDENER KNOWS THE JOY of early spring, when ten-der yellow-green shoots start breaking through soil that only recently was crusted and frozen. But that happiness pales in comparison with the ardor of the moment when, hav-ing been cultivated, weeded, and watered, the garden is in lush, full bloom.

If the road to mature discipleship has a destination, an ulti-mate goal, what is it? What would the "full bloom" of mature discipleship look like? Fr. Rolheiser writes that the answer is found in an instruction Jesus gives to his followers: "Be perfect as your heavenly Father is perfect."

This saying might strike fear into the hearts of those of us who suffer from scrupulosity. Try as we might, none of us is perfect. However, to obtain the true meaning of this teaching we must look beneath the surface. Jesus is not saying we are to slave under the taskmaster of perfectionism. It is humanly impossible for any of us to achieve perfection. Rather, he is asking us to be perfect as *our God is perfect.* Fr. Rolheiser writes that the perfection of God to which Jesus points is God's demonstration of the fullness of compassion. In effect, Jesus is saying to us, "Be compassionate as your heavenly father is compassionate."

Fr. Rolheiser explains that the compassion Jesus demands is unique:

> Jesus defines it in this way: God, he says, lets his sun shine on the bad as well as the good. God's love does not discriminate; it simply embraces everything. Like the sun, it does not shine selectively.... It just shines, and everything irrespective of its condition receives its warmth.

That means that there is literally nothing that is beyond the scope and reach of the love and compassion of God, be it the "saints in heaven" or the "devils in hell." As for humankind, God loves us when we are gloriously good and insanely bad. As believers in the God of Jesus Christ, we are called to do the same for everyone we meet.

It's a serious challenge. How can we possibly love unconditionally those who are bad as well as those who are good? Do the moral choices of others matter or not? Is it possible for us to embrace others indiscriminately in the manner of the father in the parable of the prodigal son? Fr. Rolheiser says "yes."

We do this by loving people fully even as we hold our moral ground, much in the way that parents can love their children completely even as they challenge their children's behavior. Like a parent who embraces a daughter but holds the line at her sharing a bed with her boyfriend while visiting the family home, we are invited to embrace the world with love and compassion even as we stand in the truth that our differences matter—sometimes acutely.

To be a mature disciple is to clearly see the distinctions but also to hold a place of love and compassion. It is the ability to radiate the compassion of God, a task that is not easy in the pluralistic age in which we live. Humanity is divided along countless lines, including ethnicity, race, language, religion, wealth, and culture. It is challenging to recognize as brothers and sisters people who appear to be completely different from us.

But to not do so has serious consequences, writes Fr. Rolheiser, including demonization and distrust. We find ourselves in opposition, or avoid each other to avoid the discomfort of the dissonance. We tune in the cable news station that aligns with our point of view and avoid the station that doesn't. We judge the worship styles and more of other parishes and enjoy a righteous sense that we are the ones who are Catholic in the "right" way. We break along political lines and associate only with the like-minded. We split over issues (prolife or prochoice; feminist or traditionalist) and have little patience with those who think differently.

The solution, writes Fr. Rolheiser, is found in the Gospel of John in the story of the foot washing. Unlike the synoptic Gospels of Mark, Matthew, and Luke, the centerpiece of the story of the Eucharist in John is not the consecration of the Eucharist but the act of humble service by Jesus, who takes a towel and basin and performs a task normally relegated to slaves.

This story operates upon our hearts and minds at multiple levels. On one level, we see the tables turned on social convention. The master has become the servant. Looking even more deeply, we see a particular kind of humility at work here. In the Gospel of John, which was written at the end of the first century of Christianity, communities were experiencing conflicts over the correct ways to celebrate the Eucharist. John's Gospel moves away from focusing on the institution of the great meal of remembrance to the meaning of the meal: it is about reaching each other beyond and despite the differences that separate us. In Jesus Christ, in the Eucharist, there is no divide between people.

The image is apt for our age. Fr. Rolheiser points to abortion, which is among the issues most hotly contested today. What might happen, he asks, if the prochoice and prolife groups were to meet each other first with a towel and a basin and then enter into discussion?

To follow Jesus is to be willing to manifest the expansive compassion of God that stretches us beyond bitter disagreement. Like him, we must remove our outer garment so that we can be in touch with more profound inner realities. Fr Rolheiser observes that to follow Jesus is to be willing to be naked, to lay down "specific ethnicity, language, religious identity, culture, political affiliation, ideology, set of moral judgments, and a whole gamut of private wounds and indignations" so that we can discover our real identity.

That real identity is the deep memory that we "have come from God, are returning to God, and therefore are capable of doing anything, including loving and washing the feet of someone very different from ourselves," Fr. Rolheiser notes. Knowing that every one of us is made in the image and likeness of our God is the deep truth with which mature disciples must be in touch.

The parable of the woman and the lost coin illustrates this truth. The value of the coin was insignificant; what mattered was

that without it, the woman's treasure was not whole (as represented by the number nine). Imagine a family in which there is harmony between the parents and nine of their children but a cutoff with the tenth. The family, simply put, is not whole. Only when that last person is back in the circle is wholeness achieved.

Think about the many places—families, churches, communities—where we tolerate being incomplete. Aware that we have lost people who should be with us, we righteously stand our ground, happier to hold our position than to emulate the hard work of the woman who lost the coin. But to be a mature disciple requires that we cast a gaze of compassion on all who surround us so that we can repair the fractures that separate humankind and create an unbroken circle that is truly made in the image and likeness of God.

✠ ✠ ✠

Sharing Our Faith

✠ "Whether we are Catholic or Protestant, Evangelical or Unitarian, Christian or Jew, Jew or Muslim, Christian or Muslim, prolife or prochoice, liberal or conservative, we all must find the compassion and empathy to be able to embrace in a way that expresses love and understanding even as that embrace does not say that differences are of no importance." Reflect on the tensions that Fr. Rolheiser describes. What is your reaction to this? In what ways does this challenge your spiritual growth?

✠ Martin Luther King once said "it is appalling that the most segregated hour of Christian America is eleven o'clock on Sunday morning"—meaning that, over all, the Christian church was largely divided into white and minority congregations. Is this still true? Should Christians concern themselves with this issue? Should your parish? Why or why not?

✚ Fr. Rolheiser asserts that there is nothing outside the scope and reach of the compassionate love of the God of Jesus Christ, including the "devils in hell." What is your response to this assertion?

Living the Good News

Where do you find yourself stirred by the Word of God and his presence among and within your group? What action might you take in response to this? Share with your group what you will do, within the context of your own life, to act upon what you have experienced.

We offer a few examples for you to consider here. These are just examples. You can act individually or as a group. If you find that one of them touches you, by all means use it, but you may also think of other individual or group actions that inspire you.

Fr. Rolheiser speaks of ways in which we cover our nakedness, hiding in our cultural groups, ethic circles, language, and religious identity. In what ways do you don "outer garments" like these? Write your reflection in your journal. What would it take for you to set aside something you use for protective "cover?" Consider actively letting go this week of something that protects you.

Fr. Rolheiser asserts that tragedies are moments in which humankind forgets surface differences, choosing instead to dwell in the deep reality that all of us are made in the image and likeness of God. Can you think of moments in which you've experienced this truth? Whom do you find difficult to envision as the image and likeness of God? Take time this week to learn about a community of people that are different from you. What do they reveal about God?

Today there are many ways to wash each other's feet. For instance, there are sick, homebound, and needy people in your parish or community. If there is a ministry in your parish that cares for such people, become a part of it. If there is not, be an agent for starting one.

✢ ✢ ✢

Closing Prayer

Share together prayers of intercession or praise.

Then pray this closing prayer together:

> Loving God, in you there are no separations.
> Forgive us for the ways in which we have rent
> the fabric of your reign
> with harsh judgment and pain.
> Help us see each other with your eyes,
> eyes that gaze with constant compassion and love.
> Open our hearts to do your will.
> Where we are divided, bring us together.
> Make us as energized and purposeful
> as the woman who searched for the coin
> as we work to heal the divides between your people.
> In the name of Jesus, we pray.
> Amen.

Looking Ahead

Prepare for your next session by prayerfully reading and studying Session 7. You can also supplement your preparation by reading Sacred Fire, pages 127 to 129.

Informal Gathering

Wholeness

To Live the Baptism of Jesus and Not Just of John

Sharing

Briefly share on one of the following questions:

"How am I right now?" or
"What good news would I like to share?"

Sharing the Good News

Share how you did with your action response from the last session (Living the Good News) or how you were able to incorporate the message of the last session into your daily life.

Lifting Our Hearts

... in Song

Play or sing the following song or another song of your choosing:

"River of Glory"

... in the Quiet

Pause for a few moments of silence and allow yourself to more deeply embrace the presence of God.

... in the Word

Read aloud Matthew 3:13-17

As the reader proclaims the sacred text, allow yourself to ponder a word, a phrase, a question, or a feeling that rises up from within you. Reflect on this in silence; when you are invited, briefly share it aloud with the group.

(If no one wishes to speak, simply allow the group to be enveloped in the silence, and allow the reflection to continue for a few more moments.)

... in Prayer

> God our Father,
> like a voice crying in the desert,
> John the Baptist announced that the one
> who would bring about your reign was near.
> Unafraid, John called people to turn their hearts
>   back to you and repent.
> Grant that we might have similar courage
> in proclaiming your Good News
> in our age and in all places.
> Embraced by your grace and baptized in your name,
> we trust that in you we have been given
> everything we need for this task.
> In you, we are whole and we are complete.
> We pray this in the name of our brother Jesus
> through whom the Spirit is breathed out
> upon the world.
> Amen

Our Companion on the Journey

St. John XXIII

"In the daily exercise of Our pastoral office, it sometimes happens that We hear certain opinions which disturb Us—opinions expressed by people who, though fired with a commendable zeal for religion, are lacking in sufficient prudence and judgment in their evaluation of events. They can see nothing but calamity and disaster in the present state of the world. They say over and over that this modern age of ours, in comparison with past ages, is definitely deteriorating. One would think from their attitude that history, that great teacher of life, had taught them nothing. They seem to imagine that in the days of the earlier councils everything was as it should be so far as doctrine and morality and the Church's rightful liberty were concerned.

"We feel that We must disagree with these prophets of doom, who are always forecasting worse disasters, as though the end of the world were at hand.

"Present indications are that the human family is on the threshold of a new era. We must recognize here the hand of God, who, as the years roll by, is ever directing men's efforts, whether they realize it or not, towards the fulfillment of the inscrutable designs of His providence, wisely arranging everything, even adverse human fortune, for the Church's good."

Pope St. John XXIII, address at the opening
of the Second Vatican Council, October 11, 1962

ANGELO GIUSEPPE RONCALLI was elected pope in 1958, taking the name John XXIII. Roncalli, who was born to a farming family in Sotto il Monte, Lombardy, Italy in 1881, was ordained a priest in Rome in 1904. He served as a chaplain and stretcher bearer in the Italian army during the First World War. He also held a number of diplomatic offices in the Church.

Historians believe that the cardinal electors chose him, a 76-year-old man, expecting that his pontificate would be transitional and relatively brief. Three months after his election, however, Pope John surprised the Church and the world when he called for the convening of an ecumenical council. Having lived through two world wars, the Holocaust, the spread of Communism, and the intensification of the Cold War with its escalating arms race, he was eager to see the Church preach the unchanging Gospel message in ways more relevant to the modern world, and he wanted the Church to take the lead in pursuing Christian unity.

The council, a gathering of bishops from throughout the world, produced documents addressing an amazing wide spectrum of topics including the reform of the liturgy, the Church's relationship with other religions, the nature of the office of the bishop and priest, the rights of human persons, the use of modern communication, and much more. The impact of the Council is still being felt.

John XXIII is also remembered for two landmark encyclicals, *Mater et Magistra (Mother and Teacher)* and *Pacem in Terris (Peace on Earth)*.

Mater et Magistra (Mother and Teacher), issued in 1961, addressed the social and economic changes in the seventy years since Pope Leo XIII issued the encyclical *Rerum Novarum*—the first modern papal pronouncement on economic and social issues. *Mater et Magistra* addressed many such issues, including the need for a just wage, the primacy of private initiative, the right of individuals to play a role in community life, the proper balance between the role of government and the rights of individuals, and the obligation of public authorities to prevent upheavals such as mass unemployment. *Pacem in Terris (Peace on Earth)*, issued in 1963, challenged world leaders on fundamental human rights, the common good, and the escalating arms race.

The goal of John XXIII was an updating of the ministry of the Church in response to the scientific, economic, social, and political changes that had occurred over the previous seven decades. The impact of the forces unleashed during his tenure as the bishop of Rome is still unfolding, but it is safe to say that this holy, joyful, and visionary pope was anything but a "place holder" during his five years in the See of St. Peter. He died in 1963, before the council concluded, and he was canonized in 2014.

Encountering Wisdom for Life

JOHN THE BAPTIST IS ONE OF THE MOST vivid figures in the Gospels. The cousin of Jesus, he stands in the long prophetic tradition of Israel as he cries out, echoing the words of Isaiah, "I am 'the voice of one crying out in the desert. Make straight the way of the Lord!'" (John 1:23). Many of the people who go to John, hear his preaching, and are baptized by him in the Jordan River wonder who he is. Is he the promised Messiah? Clearly, he is renowned enough to be perceived as a threat, imprisoned, and martyred by Herod Antipas, the tetrarch of Galilee.

The baptism of John is seen as an act of repentance by those who come to him. John himself proclaims that he is not the Messiah; one will come after him with a gift far greater. That gift is the sacramental baptism that we recognize as conferring forgiveness of sins as well as the renewal of the entire human person. In that baptism we are incorporated into the very life of Jesus and become part of the Body of Christ, the Church.

Fr. Rolheiser explains why John's baptism is incomplete. "It can denounce a king by showing what is wrong," he notes, "and it can wash the soul in sand by blasting off accumulated rust and dirt; but ultimately, it cannot empower us to correct anything." In other words, we do not become whole simply because we feel sorrow about what we have done. In Fr. Rolheiser's words, "Something else is needed." That something is given to us in the baptism of Jesus, which not only reveals where we are called to repent but gives us the power to become changed people.

Each of us has felt remorse and has wanted to change. And we might even know what we need to do in order to change. Take for example the issue of being overweight. If we were to poll 100 people about how they might reduce their weight, almost to a person they would say, "Eat less, and exercise more." Everyone knows this simple plan will lead to a leaner body. Still, the National Institutes of Health report that more than two thirds of adults are either overweight or obese. Clearly, knowing something and having the power to act on that knowledge are two different things.

So, too, with addiction. We live in an age rife with addictive behaviors involving alcohol, drugs, the internet, gambling, video gaming, and pornography. When these behaviors prove problematic, eroding relationships and putting them at risk, the addict may long to change, but meaningful, lasting change happens only when the person is willing to move beyond the use of willpower and, in a community of recovering people, embrace a new way of living. A spiritual solution is needed. The key is welcoming and surrendering to the healing grace of God which, one day at a time, helps addicted persons do what they could not do before.

Fr. Rolheiser writes that our job is to live the baptism of Jesus and not just that of John. The baptism of John illuminates what is wrong and calls on us to resolve to change our behavior. But the baptism of Jesus enfolds us in the arms of a grace-filled community, empowering us to do what we cannot do with our will alone.

It sounds too good to be true. But that is the abundance of our God. God's grace is not magic; grace is the self-gift of God. It comes to us freely, even when we think it is undeserved. Washed in God's grace at baptism, we become the children of God, capable of following him. And through the grace of baptism, we are empowered to work for the fullness of God's reign in the world—a reign we believe is "already and not yet."

Ultimately, grace is a mystery, not something that we can scientifically prove. Fr. Rolheiser writes that the only empirical evidence we get for the existence of grace is that we see its fruit.

It is so heartening to let in the vast power of God's love and self-gift. There is no need for us to rely only on the baptism of John. As followers of Jesus, as mature disciples, we can find in God's grace a strength that transcends all understanding. Perhaps this is why the hymn "Amazing Grace," with all that it affirms, is so beloved by Christians.

✠ ✠ ✠

Sharing Our Faith

✦ In the Gospels, Jesus tells his followers that it is easier for a rich person to pass through the eye of a needle than to enter heaven. They cry out, "then it's impossible!" Scholars debate about whether the "eye of a needle" is a reference to an actual awl used for sewing or a very small gate into the city that no camel could have passed through while burdened with baggage. However you understand it, the point is that the one who has everything has to surrender a lot in order to enter the kingdom of heaven. Examine your life as it is now. What would you have to give up to pass through the needle's eye? Possessions? Judgments? Activities? What are the dangers of various forms of wealth in our lives today?

✦ John the Baptist is a powerful evangelist. He's also a bit strange, attired in animal skins, living in the desert, and eating locusts. Who are the people you listen to and who shape your understanding and faith? Do people have to appear a certain way or have specific credentials for you to take them seriously? What would you do if you encountered a modern-day John the Baptist in the pews of your place of worship?

✦ What is your understanding of grace? The *Catechism of the Catholic Church* offers many beautiful descriptions, among them favor, participation in the life of God, gratuitous gift, and a sanctifying and justifying gift. Is grace too good to be true? Where do you see the grace of God at work in your life?

Living the Good News

Where do you find yourself stirred by the Word of God and his presence among and within your group? What action might you take in response to this? Share with your group what you will do, within the context of your own life, to act upon what you have experienced.

We offer a few examples for you to consider here. You can act individually or as a group. If you find that one of these examples touches you, by all means use it, but you may also think of other individual or group actions that inspire you.

Spend time with someone who is recovering from an addiction. Interview the person about what the words "surrender" and "grace" mean to him or her. Write in your journal about your reactions. In your prayer, ask God to help you open yourself to the grace you need to face a challenge in your life.

Take time to think and pray about the meaning of baptism in your life. Attend a baptism in your parish and listen carefully—as though for the first time—to the words of the rite. What stands out for you?

Do you make it a practice to recognize God's grace—to thank God for his presence and gifts? The writer Anne LaMott claims that there are only three prayers: "Help," "Thanks," and "Wow!" This week, use these three in moments when you are conscious of grace, are grateful for graces bestowed, or are in awe of God's gracious goodness.

✠ ✠ ✠

Closing Prayer

Share together prayers of intercession or praise.
Then pray this closing prayer together:

> Loving God,
> your goodness is vast and your generosity unbounded.
> We thank you for the graces you shower upon us,

graces noticed and unnoticed,
graces merited and unearned.
Help us, like Pope St. John XXIII,
to trust your presence completely.
Enable us to turn our lives and our will over to you,
to turn to you whenever we feel alone
    or burdened.
We trust that you are at the ready
to come to us in our need.
In the name of Jesus, we pray.
Amen.

Looking Ahead

*Prepare for your next session by prayerfully reading and studying
Session 8. You can also supplement your preparation by reading*
Sacred Fire, *pages 129 to 133.*

Informal Gathering

SESSION 8

Patience

Waiting in the Upper Room

Sharing

Briefly share on one of the following questions:

"How am I right now?" or
"What good news would I like to share?"

Sharing the Good News

Share how you did with your action response from the last session (Living the Good News) or how you were able to incorporate the message of the last session into your daily life.

Lifting Our Hearts

... in Song

Play or sing the following song or another song of your choosing:

"We Come to Your Feast"

... in the Quiet

Pause for a few moments of silence and allow yourself to more deeply embrace the presence of God.

... in the Word

Read aloud Luke 24:33-49

As the reader proclaims the sacred text, allow yourself to ponder a word, a phrase, a question, or a feeling that rises up from within you. Reflect on this in silence; when you are invited, briefly share it aloud with our group.

(If no one wishes to speak, simply allow the group to be enveloped in the silence, and allow the reflection to continue for a few more moments.)

... in Prayer

> Loving God,
> you are the one who created darkness and light,
> who made this world and everything in it.
> Seeing what you had done
> you called it "good."
> Help us remember that we, too,
> are your beloved creation.
> Help us remember that you are always with us
> even when the challenges of life
> cause us to tremble with fear
> or sink with depression.
> Help us feel your presence
> when we are filled with gratitude
> or standing in the midst of the dark night
> of the soul.
> For we believe that your faithfulness is great
> and your promises are true.
> In Jesus' name we pray.
> Amen.

Our Companion on the Journey

St. Thérèse of Lisieux

"I know of one means only by which to attain to perfection: LOVE. Let us love, since our heart is made for
nothing else. Sometimes I seek another word to express
Love, but in this land of exile 'the word which begins
and ends' (St. Augustine) is quite incapable of render-
ing the vibrations of the soul; we must then adhere to
this simple and only word:

TO LOVE.

But on whom shall our poor heart lavish its love? Who
shall be found that is great enough to be the recipient of
its treasures? Will a human being know how to comprehend them, and above all will he be able to repay?
There exists but one Being capable of comprehending
love; it is Jesus; He alone can give us back infinitely
more than we shall ever give to him."

St. Thérèse of Lisieux

S T. THÉRÈSE OF LISIEUX was a Carmelite nun who
lived in France during the late 19th century.
Known for her strong determination, Thérèse
was driven by a passion for God from the time of
her childhood. At the age of fifteen, she pleaded
with her bishop to allow her to enter consecrated
life. Moved by her entreaties, the bishop gave her
permission to join the Carmelite community in
Lisieux.

Jansenism, which claimed that human nature
was so depraved as to be incapable of good, had
been formally condemned in the 18th century;
however, a sort of religious scrupulosity persisted.

Thérèse and many of her sisters suffered under this notion, believing that given their fallen state, none could possibly attain heaven.

An overwhelming sense of peace, however, came over Thérèse upon her profession of vows. In that moment, she saw herself as no less loved and accepted by God than all the other parts of God's wonderful creation. She came to passionately believe that as long as she sought him, Jesus would delight in her, his "little flower."

In her prayer and in her life, Thérèse began to seek what she called "a little way," and she wrote about what she found. She deepened into a great mystic, offering both her joys and trials to God. She died at aged 24, was canonized and later named a doctor of the Church. Her autobiography, *Story of a Soul*, has helped countless faithful people to recognize that living an ordinary life, in which one is conscious of God's will and faithfully tries to do it, can be a path of great holiness.

St. Thérèse was a visionary. Almost 75 years later, the Second Vatican Council would affirm her belief that all of humanity experiences what the council fathers called "the universal call to holiness." As St. Thérèse noted, "Holiness consists simply in doing God's will, and being just what God wants us to be," something that is possible for all believers.

SESSION 8

Encountering Wisdom for Life

PETER MAURIN, WHO CO-FOUNDED the Catholic Worker movement with Dorothy Day, once told her, "When you don't know what else to do, keep going to meetings, because Pentecost happened at a meeting!" That counsel might jar those of us who have spent more hours than we care to admit sitting around tables or in carefully laid-out rows discussing community, school, or church issues. Meetings today hardly feel sacred.

But, as Maurin implied, it is often in a gathering of people that the Spirit of God exerts its influence. In the conclusion of Luke's Gospel, right before Jesus ascends to his Father, he gives his followers an instruction: "Stay in the city until you are clothed with power from on high." Despite the terrible uncertainty they felt, they stayed together in community, trusting that something would happen. As they were gathered together as the community of believers, the Spirit came to the disciples in the midst of their fear, anxiety, and depression. As Fr. Rolheiser reiterates, Pentecost happened at a meeting; it did not happen to solitary individuals.

We can learn a lot from the vivid picture of the community huddled in the upper room. Many of us struggle to stay strong of heart and remain committed to our faith communities. The scandals of recent years have left some of us feeling disillusioned, discouraged by the behavior of leaders who prioritized concern about the Church's image over the protection of vulnerable children or the accountability of those who had harmed them. Like the disciples, we may no longer feel sure or confident about staying in a community that has let us down. Or we may stay, but we may feel deflated, lacking the energy or drive we once had. Our batteries are depleted, and we see no source of renewal.

In addition to this kind of disillusionment, there is a broader phenomenon affecting the Catholic Church, other Christian communities, and other faith traditions. Fr. Rolheiser describes a "hardening secularity" that surrounds us in which it is becoming more difficult for people to pass on their faith and values, "to fire the religious and romantic imagination of their culture." Church attendance, for example, is down, and agnosticism is on the rise. Families see their children living their lives comfortably indifferent to participation in religious life.

What is the answer? "Return to the city and remain in the upper room!" writes Fr. Rolheiser. In the Gospels, Jerusalem is not merely a geographic location. It is the holy and symbolic center of the faith of Israel, the location of the Temple, the dwelling place of God. When the two travelers turned away from the site of the crucifixion and headed home to Emmaus, when they turned their backs on Jerusalem, they also turned their backs on the community of believers who had followed Jesus and the dream of deliverance through the Messiah.

For those two discouraged travelers to change direction and go back to Jerusalem, to return to the city, was to reawaken their commitment and to embrace their faith in Jesus once again. For each of us, too, there comes a time when we are called to reawaken and recommit to our "faith dream," no matter how fearful or downtrodden we may be. We are often called to do this despite our circumstances and in the face of evidence that is telling us to give up.

To make this journey, we must join other believers in our own version of an upper room. This could be a small faith-sharing group, a prayer group, a Bible-study group, or a parish organization. It could be this faith-sharing group. Some of our upper rooms will be found in kitchens, living rooms and parish halls and meeting rooms, where we gather with others in faith to pray and to commit ourselves to being the mature disciples Christ calls us to be.

Fr. Rolheiser notes that most of our upper rooms—including the humble site in which the disciples gathered—are not fancy.

They don't look as glorious as the painting of the Last Supper by Leonardo da Vinci with its banquet spread and a serene vista through the open window. In fact, our upper rooms may be found in basements—with rickety folding chairs, florescent light fixtures, and disposable coffee cups. Still, the believer who struggles today need only pull a chair up to the table and sit, to join the group and trust. The advice is the same more than 2000 years later: "Stay in the city until you are clothed with power from on high." Because, after all, "Pentecost happened at a meeting."

Sharing Our Faith

✠ To those who knew her, St. Thérèse of Lisieux seemed like a very ordinary person. She had great humility and saw herself as the "Little Flower of Jesus," much like the humble wildflowers of the forest or field. How do you see yourself? Do you compare yourselves to others? Who? Are your judgements of yourself harsh or generous? What would you do differently if you were following the example of St. Thérèse? In what ways does "ordinary" discipleship have the potential to be something extraordinary?

✠ We might be tempted to compare our discipleship today to the discipleship of the followers of Jesus who knew him when he was alive, and think that they, having seen him, had it easier. And yet, those disciples were human beings, and they experienced the same challenges of faith and trust that we do. What feelings do you think gripped those gathered in the upper room? Why do you think Jesus instructed them to return to Jerusalem? Have you ever had a similar experience of faith? If you have, what did you learn from it?

✠ What meetings do you attend? Why do you go to them? Do you think of them as "upper rooms"? Why or why not? If not, what would it take for you to shift your perspective and see meetings as Pentecost opportunities?

Living the Good News

Where do you find yourself stirred by the Word of God and his presence among and within your group? What action might you take in response to this? Share with your group what you will do, within the context of your own life, to act upon what you have experienced.

We offer a few suggestions for you to consider here. These are just suggestions. You can act individually or as a group. If you find that

one of them touches you, by all means use it, but you may also think
of other individual or group actions that inspire you.

🌐 In the next week, notice what happens every time you
are gathered with two or more people. What are you
doing? Do you find this time life giving? If not, what
would it take to make the meetings you go to life giving?

🌐 When bad news about the Church is reported in the secular media, it may be hard to keep heart. It is a challenge
to evangelize when public opinion is against you. But
this was the situation in which the first followers of Jesus
found themselves. Do you know anyone who is experiencing some form of the "dark night of the soul"? Have
you shared your faith with this person? Have you listened
to him or her with your heart? This week, reach out to
someone who would be blessed by your attention or com-
panionship.

🌐 After attending Mass or participating in a prayerful meeting, discern what you feel the Spirit is asking you to do,
and act on it.

✛ ✛ ✛

Closing Prayer

Share prayers of intercession or praise.

Then pray this closing prayer together:

> Creator God,
> you love us in the midst of our joys
> and the depth of our sorrows.
> You lift us when our strength is gone
> and carry us forward when we feel we can no longer

move on.
Help us to stay aware of your presence,
to trust that your arms are around us
in an embrace of acceptance and love.
Love us when we cannot love ourselves
and sustain us when we find ourselves in desert times.
In the name of Jesus, we pray.
Amen.

Looking Ahead

*Prepare for your next session by prayerfully reading and studying
Session 9. You can also supplement your preparation by reading*
Sacred Fire, *pages 133 to 144.*

Informal Gathering

Goodness to Greatness

The Invitation to the Rich Young Man

Sharing

Briefly share on one of the following questions:

"How am I right now?" or
"What good news would I like to share?"

Sharing the Good News

Share how you did with your action response from the last session (Living the Good News) or how you were able to incorporate the message of the last session into your daily life.

Lifting Our Hearts

... in Song

Play or sing the following song or another song of your choosing:

"I Am for You"

... in the Quiet

Pause for a few moments of silence, and allow yourself to more deeply embrace the presence of God.

... in the Word

Read aloud Matthew 19: 16-30

As the reader proclaims the sacred text, allow yourself to ponder a word, a phrase, a question, or a feeling that rises up from within you. Reflect on this in silence; when you are invited, briefly share it aloud with our group.

If no one wishes to speak, simply allow the group to be enveloped in the silence, and allow the reflection to continue for a few more moments.

... in Prayer

> God our Father,
> You gave us the law and prophets
> to illumine our path to you.
> Over and over, we turned away.
> Like the rich young man,
> we were blinded by the things of the world.
> Your Son came, drawing us fully to himself
> and bringing to fulfillment your reign.
> Open our hearts to see
> where we have fallen short
> in following him.
> Draw us back to you
> so that we may see what treasure truly is.
> In you all things are possible.
> In the name of Jesus, we pray. Amen.

Our Companion on the Journey

The Church Women of El Salvador

"The Peace Corps left today and my heart sank low. The danger is extreme and they were right to leave... Now I

must assess my own position, because I am not up for
suicide. Several times I have decided to leave
El Salvador. I almost could, except for the children, the
poor, bruised victims of this insanity. Who would care
for them? Whose heart could be so staunch as to favor
the reasonable thing in a sea of their tears and loneliness? Not mine, dear friend, not mine."

Jean Donovan, letter to a friend

IN THE EARLY CENTURIES OF THE CHURCH, people
understood that they might be martyred for
their faith; the empire was hostile to the emergent
Church. But today, many Christians never have to
give martyrdom a second thought. Many, but not
all.

On December 2, 1980, four women working as missionaries in El Salvador were beaten,
raped, and murdered by plain-clothed members
of the Salvadoran National Guard. The women's
bodies were buried in a shallow grave. Ursuline
Sister Dorothy Kazel, Maryknoll lay missioner
Jean Donovan, and Maryknoll Sisters Ita Ford and
Maura Clarke were singled out for teaching the
faith, providing pastoral care for those in need,
and particularly for trying to protect poor refugees
from the Salvadoran civil war.

Inspired by the preaching of Archbishop Oscar
Romero (who was beatified on May 23, 2015),
the women had remained in El Salvador despite
increasing violence. They believed their day-to-day
work with those who were poor and displaced was
too critical to abandon.

Their fate was shared by thousands of unnamed
people who "disappeared" in El Salvador. These

peasants lived in constant terror of being kid-
napped and murdered. In 1980 alone, 10,000
Salvadoran citizens were killed.

The murder of the women was met with public
outrage. American citizens demanded that their
government pressure the government of
El Salvador to investigate the crimes. After a
whitewashing review by Salvadoran authorities
that was abetted by some U.S. government offi-
cials, the United Nations initiated a Commission
on Truth for El Salvador. This group revealed that
the orders given to the soldiers came from high in
the Salvadoran military and that there had been
tens of thousands of murders, abductions, incidents
of torture, and other crimes during the civil war.
These revelations ignited an intense debate about
U.S. policy toward El Salvador. Six people were
eventually convicted of murdering the women:
four soldiers and two generals.

The deaths of the church women proved to be
a turning point for El Salvador. The sacrifice those
women made brought about a critical awareness
that enabled some justice to be done for the name-
less thousands who were murdered and never
found. Truly, Dorothy, Jean, Ita, and Maura met
the ultimate conditions for discipleship: "Whoever
does not take up his cross and follow after me is
not worthy of me. Whoever finds his life will lose
it, and whoever loses his life for my sake will find
it" (Matthew 10:38-39).

SESSION 9

Encountering Wisdom for Life

ANAGEMENT CONSULTANT JIM COLLINS wrote a book that reported how certain companies had been able to transition from being merely average to being industry leaders. The book, *Good to Great*, has sold more than four million copies. Small surprise: Business people of all types, from corporate innovators to leaders in the social sector, are eager to find out the recipe for success.

When it comes to discipleship, though, many of us are not interested in going to any length to achieve greatness; we're happy to settle for "average." Rather than seeing the exceptional followers of Jesus in our age as providing a path we can emulate, many are more comfortable placing them on a pedestal, rationalizing that we could never be so holy, so giving, so prayerful. "I'm no Mother Teresa," many would say. "I'm no Oscar Romero."

The four women martyred in El Salvador were not trying to be saints; they were doing what they felt they had been called to do—caring for people who were poor and powerless. Often, we are more comfortable with a personal spirituality than with a spirituality that calls us into action.

Fr. Rolheiser writes that every one of us has the potential to move from being "a saint in progress to a saint in actuality." If so, why is it that there seem to be only a few "standout" disciples in each generation? What must we do to take our maturity as disciples beyond the ordinary to a much higher level? The answer, he writes, is found in a gospel story that illuminates what it takes to be a great disciple.

In the story we commonly call "the rich young man," we see someone who is basically a very good person invited by Jesus to take the next step. Unlike other people Jesus encounters who are separated from the community (Zacchaeus, Levi, the woman caught in adultery), the rich young man seems to be a member

103

in good standing. He is solid in his faith. He is honest, decent, and knowledgeable about what his tradition—Judaism—asks of him. When he inquires of Jesus what he must do to have eternal life, the answer is, effectively, be a devout Jew: Keep the commandments. And for good measure, Jesus lists a few of them.

The young man must have been happy to hear that answer, as he explains that he has, in fact, observed these commandments. Well, then, says Jesus, if you wish to be perfect—if you want to be not just good but great in your faith, then go sell everything you have, give to the poor, and follow me. This seems like too much to ask, so the crestfallen man leaves Jesus. He cannot imagine doing what Jesus asks.

Too often and much like the rich young man of the story, we bristle or feel despondent when we are challenged to share our resources. The United States is one of the wealthiest countries in the world. Even so, millions of people in the United States, including many families with children, live below the poverty line. Our Catholic faith calls us to live our lives aware of and of service to those that are most vulnerable, and to work to change systems that keep people oppressed and unequal. Why is it that we are not in action every day to address this challenge as people of faith?

Fr. Rolheiser offers a story that illuminates what it means for us to follow in the manner Jesus asks of the rich young man. Once, Fr. Rolheiser was leading a retreat for priests. After the evening concluded, he was invited to join some of them in what they described as a "support-group meeting." There, the priests took turns sharing with each other the many ways they had failed in their ministry. With candor and depth, they described for each other the things that had stymied them in living up to what is demanded of the followers of Christ. They spoke of such things as shortcomings in caring for those in need, resentments, anger, and self-involvement.

Fr. Rolheiser had never experienced anything quite like this, so afterward, the founder of the group explained the group's genesis. Overworked by the demands of leading and serving four rural parishes, the priest founder had become exhausted and angry, the price of trying to do too much. Although he maintained a good façade and was loved by the people in the parishes, he found himself getting more and more righteously self-indulgent. He saw fine food, fine wine, and first-class vacations as appropriate rewards for all of his sacrifices. Slowly and somewhat unconsciously, he allowed these "perqs" to become a dominant force in his life. He was a good priest, the man explained, but he was clearly not a great one: His discipleship and sacrifice went only so far.

Then his father, who was much admired, died. As the priest grieved that loss, the depths of his sadness brought forth a gift. Reflecting on his father's life and all that he had accomplished personally and professionally, the young priest realized that if he was going to be a priest, then he was not going to settle for being a mediocre one; he was going to be a great one.

The priest realized that to change his life, to rid himself of the willingness to settle for simply being good and lavishly rewarding himself for his sacrifices, he could not rely on willpower alone. He would need the grace that comes through community. So the priest asked his best friends to join him on a journey of transparency. They would pray together, and they also would be rigorously honest with each other about their lives and their success in following Jesus.

To follow Jesus is to admit the truth about what we are doing with the gifts we have been given, whether that's our time, our talent, or our treasure—as our parish stewardship invitations remind us every year. Some of us will be asked to have the courage and commitment to leave home and security to serve those in need—like the women of El Salvador and countless others. Others of us will be responsible to see the places of inequity and poverty right in our own towns and cities—even in our own parishes.

The good news is that while Jesus is telling us that to truly live in the reign of God we can hold back nothing, he doesn't ask us to go it alone. Like the priests in the support group, we can achieve the deepest levels of surrender to God's plan for us when we support each other and are accountable to each other. Only then is the deep joy that every person longs for a possibility. In the words of Fr. Rolheiser, "We become saints only with the help of others."

Fr. Rolheiser writes that this decision—how much we are truly willing to give ourselves and everything we have to God— is the difference between being a good disciple and being a great disciple. Every day we meet with the challenge described by the faithful priest at the retreat: Will we give all of our "rooms" to God?

✢ ✢ ✢

Sharing Our Faith

✠ Think about the lives of the church women of El Salvador who made the ultimate sacrifice to continue following the call of Christ. What do you see in them? How are they like the rich young man? How are they different?

✠ What role do you think community played in the decision of the church women of El Salvador to continue to accompany the suffering people in spite of personal danger? What kinds of sacrifices have you made for friends, neighbors and strangers who were suffering? In what ways is action on behalf of others central to the Christian life?

✠ Fr. Rolheiser asks us to aim to not only be good about our faith but great in its practice. What are the practices that support your spiritual life? In what ways are you strong? In what ways do you need improvement? Have you ever taken a bold action in support of the poor? What was it? How did you feel before, during, and after? How did your experience impact subsequent actions?

Living the Good News

Where do you find yourself stirred by the Word of God and his presence among and within your group? What action might you take in response to this? Share with your group what you will do, within the context of your own life, to act upon what you have experienced.

We offer a few examples for you to consider here. These are just suggestions. You can act individually or as a group. If you find that one of them touches you, by all means use it, but you may also think of other individual or group actions that inspire you.

A Catholic parish in Arizona made it an annual practice to look at its life and ministry through a particular lens. Rather than celebrating everything they did right, the parishioners spent time naming the things in the past year that fell short. These ranged from petty issues such as gossip to more serious issues such as failures to meet the needs of people who were depending on them. Consider proposing a time of reflection and evaluation for a group of which you are a part. Make a serious effort to address those issues or change those practices.

Fr. Rolheiser recounts a story drawn from the lives of the Desert Fathers. "Abbot Lot went to see Abbot Joseph and said: `Father, according as I am able, I keep my little rule, and my little fast, my prayer, meditation and contemplative silence; and according as I am able I strive to cleanse my heart of bad thoughts: now what more should I do?' The elder rose up in reply and stretched out his hands to heaven, and his fingers became like lamps of fire. He said: `Why not become all flame?'" What does the poetic phrase "all flame" mean to you? Have you ever met someone who is "all flame?" Who was it? What qualities did that person have? If that person is still alive, connect with him or her in some way, even if it is simply to affirm your impression.

This week, aim to improve an area of your spiritual practice that needs attention. Many people do a daily inventory of how they have lived each day, such as "the examen of consciousness" developed by St. Ignatius. Consider adding this practice to your life. (For more information, visit http://www.ignatianspirituality.com/ignatian-prayer/the-examen/consciousness-examen). As you review your day, pay particular attention to how your discipleship is

impacting the poor. Commit to doing something in service
to those in need that puts your faith into action this week.

 In Matthew 26:11, Jesus says, "The poor you will always
have with you, but you will not always have me."
Sometimes, people cite this Scripture to take themselves
off the hook from working to counteract poverty—as if
Jesus is somehow normalizing its presence. In fact, Jesus
was referencing Deuteronomy 15:11, which calls for
action on behalf of the poor. Take time this week to find
out how your parish and diocese are serving the needs in
your area. What can you do to support those efforts?

✠ ✠ ✠

Closing Prayer

Share together prayers of intercession or praise.

Then pray this closing prayer together:

> Lord of all, you showed us the path of life.
> You invited us to follow you
> and to walk in your ways.
> You promised that if we could give ourselves
>   fully to you,
> our share in your abundant life would be complete.
> Help us when our considerations stop us.
> Relieve us of the fear of surrendering
> to your love and your path.
> Open our hearts to handing over to you
> all of our earthly lives
> so that someday we might inherit eternal life with you.
> We pray this in the name of Jesus.
> Amen.

Looking Ahead

Prepare for your next session by prayerfully reading and studying Session 10. You can also supplement your preparation by reading Sacred Fire, *pages 144 to 166.*

Informal Gathering

The Invitation to Ponder

Mary as the Paradigm of Maturity and Discipleship

Sharing

Briefly share on one of the following questions:

"How am I right now?" or
"What good news would I like to share?"

Sharing the Good News

Share how you did with your action response from the last session (Living the Good News) or how you were able to incorporate the message of the last session into your daily life.

Lifting Our Hearts ...

... in Song

Play or sing the following song or another song of your choosing:

"We Have Been Told"

... in the Quiet

Pause for a few moments of silence and allow yourself to more deeply embrace the presence of God.

... in the Word

Read aloud Luke 1:26-38

As the reader proclaims the sacred text, allow yourself to ponder a word, a phrase, a question, or a feeling that rises up from within you. Reflect on this in silence; when you are invited, briefly share it aloud with our group.

(If no one wishes to speak, simply allow the group to be enveloped in the silence, and allow the reflection to continue for a few more moments.)

... in Prayer

Loving God,
you invited into your plan of salvation
a humble and innocent young woman.
In the face of her fear
and gripped by unknowing,
she surrendered to your will
and accepted your plans for her.
In the trials and challenges of life,
she continued to live this "yes,"
pondering in her heart
the things she encountered in her life.
Help us to be as open as Mary our Mother.
Help your Church to model her humility and wonder.
In Jesus' name we pray. Amen.

Our Companion on the Journey

Maximilian Kolbe

"Never be afraid of loving the Blessed Virgin too much.
You can never love her more than Jesus did."

Maximilian Kolbe

MAXIMILIAN KOLBE IS ONE of the many saints who lived under the constant influence of Mary, the mother of Jesus.

A priest of German and Polish lineage, he was imprisoned for agitating against the Nazis. When ten inmates were chosen to die by starvation in retribution for the escape of three prisoners, Father Kolbe offered to take the place of one man who was weeping for his wife and children. After the other nine had died, the Nazis killed Father Kolbe with an injection of carbolic acid.

When he was 12, Raymond Kolbe (his birth name) experienced an apparition of Mary.

"That night," he later wrote, "I asked the Mother of God what was to become of me. Then she came to me holding two crowns—one white, the other red. She asked me if I was willing to accept either of these crowns. The white one meant that I should persevere in purity, and the red that I should become a martyr. I said that I would accept them both."

He was ordained a Conventual Franciscan priest in 1918 and eventually earned doctorates in philosophy and theology. Through his time as a student, he promoted the concept of consecrating and entrusting one's life to Mary.

He was particularly devoted to the idea of the Immaculate Conception. When he organized a movement in Rome to work for the conversion of overt enemies of the Church and other sinners, he called it the Militia Immaculata. When he returned to Poland, he promoted veneration of Mary, founding a monthly publication called "Knight of the

Immaculate." In 1927, after operating a religious press for four years, he founded a monastery, the City of Immaculate, near Warsaw, that become a major publisher of religious material.

After missionary work in Asia and India, he returned to Poland in 1936 and, in 1938, started a radio station. He stayed in the monastery when Germany invaded Poland. After he was arrested briefly and then released, he and his few remaining colleagues sheltered refugees including about two thousand Jews. He also continued publishing religious works and material critical of the Nazis until German authorities shut down the monastery and sent Father Kolbe and four others to Auschwitz.

Encountering Wisdom for Life

D ISCIPLES WHO WANT TO MOVE from being simply "good" followers of Jesus to being truly "great" followers of Jesus find a paradigm of maturity and discipleship in Mary, the Mother of God. While many of the people who are trying to follow Jesus don't understand him, Mary stands out as someone who seems to "singularly get it right." Unlike the disciples who seem to be, at times, fearful, confused, or even a hindrance, Mary's posture of presence and pondering is something very different.

At first glance, we may think of Mary as a cinematic extra who is secondary to figures like Peter and others. The Gospels themselves may have shaped this impression. For example, in the Gospel of Matthew, when someone informs Jesus that his mother and family are looking for him, he answers, "Who is my mother? Who are my brothers and sisters?" In the Gospel of Luke, a woman cries out, blessing the womb that carried him and the breasts at which he nursed. Jesus response is a correction: "Rather, blessed are those who hear the word of God and observe it."

Fr. Rolheiser explains that we miss the point if we read these texts at a superficial level. Rather than seeing them as dismissive, we can choose to interpret them as Jesus pointing to a much deeper reality regarding Mary and a more inclusive reality regarding us. Jesus is downplaying her role as a biological instrument or a matriarch in order to intensify the focus on her faith. Fr. Rolheiser writes, "When he states that whoever hears and keeps the word of God is his true mother and brother and sister, the first person whom he is naming is his own mother, given that she was the first person to hear the word of God and fully keep it."

The secret to following Mary in pursuit of great discipleship is found in that phrase: She pondered. Where others acted or reacted, Mary reflected deeply upon the circumstances at hand, whether that was being surrounded by shepherds or finding her missing child sitting in the Temple with the rabbis.

Pondering has a particular meaning in the Hebrew sense as compared with the Greek sense. For the Greeks, the meaning is akin to examination. That remains our commonplace understanding, that pondering is simply some form of extended and focused thinking, perhaps more interior than aloud. The classic image would be the statue of "The Thinker" by the sculptor Auguste Rodin.

Pondering in the Hebrew sense had a more multivalent meaning. "Simply put, to ponder, in the Hebrew sense, meant to hold, carry, and transform tension so as not to give it back in kind, knowing that whatever energies we do not transform we will transmit," explains Fr. Rolheiser.

The image of Mary standing at the foot of the cross, gazing upon the ravaged body of her son, contains the essence of pondering. While she is mute, she is not passive. She stands there in strong witness. She is not caught up in giving way to the emotions of the moment, including the hatred and outrage that might be expected at that moment. Instead, in her silence, she is "radiating all that is antithetical to crucifixion: gentleness, understanding, forgiveness, peace, light, and courage."

To be present, to stand in witness, to let in the magnitude of what is happening without responding in kind is to truly be a great disciple. We have an example in Sr. Helen Prejean who has recounted the complexity and devastation of the death penalty in the United States in her book *Dead Man Walking*. As Patrick Sonnier was preparing to be put to death for the murder of two teenagers, a crime to which he had confessed, Sr. Helen asked him if he wanted her to be present at his execution. He said, "Yes." She then said to him, "I want the last thing in this world you see to be the face of love. You look at me." As Sonnier was strapped into the oak electric chair in the state prison in Angola, Louisiana, he looked at the father of victim David LeBlanc and asked his forgiveness. He then looked at Sr. Helen and said, "I love you." She reached out her arm from where she was standing behind the glass wall separating the gallery from the execution chamber and looked into his eyes. "I love you, too," she answered. That willingness to stand in compassion, to let in the moment, to witness to something else beyond the violence, was a moment of pondering.

The power of Mary's pondering is not to be underestimated. It is something that transforms what it encounters, absorbing the negative and demonstrating another way of being. Fr. Rolheiser uses the metaphor of a filter, which doesn't just allow water to pass through it but changes the water by removing toxins and other impurities. Certainly that was what Sr. Helen offered as she gazed into the eyes of those who have been put to death for their crimes.

This is demonstrated at its deepest and most powerful level in the death of Jesus. Fr. Rolheiser writes:

"He took in hatred, held it, transformed it, and gave back love; he took in bitterness, held it, transformed it, and gave back graciousness; he took in curses, held them, transformed them, and gave back forgiveness. Jesus resisted the instinct to give back in kind, hatred for hatred, curses for curses, jealousy for jealousy, murder for murder. He held and transformed these things rather than simply re-transmitting them. He took away the sins of the world by absorbing them, at great cost to his self."

In the sacrificial death of Jesus and in the pondering of Mary we see a path to greatness as disciples. Our job is to see their actions and embody them in our own lives. We are invited to take in the sin that is around us and, in resisting, transform the tension within our communities into peace. We may not do this perfectly, but we can try.

✤ ✤ ✤

Sharing Our Faith

✤ Bearing witness is transformative, as demonstrated by the Blessed Mother at the foot of the cross. When truth-and-reconciliation groups convene, their primary task is to listen and witness. This was true in South Africa after apartheid, in Rwanda after the genocide, and in listening sessions held to address the abuse and degradation of indigenous people in Canada. Why is witness so powerful? Where in your own life or the life of your parish could this sort of pondering be effective? What would make you willing to take such action?

✠ What is your relationship with Mary? Do you pray the rosary or say special prayers to her, such as the Hail Mary? How do you think having a deeper relationship with Mary might impact your discipleship?

✠ Have you ever been called to ponder? Share your story.

Living the Good News

Where do you find yourself stirred by the Word of God and his presence among and within your group? What action might you take in response to this? Share with your group what you will do, within the context of your own life, to act upon what you have experienced.

We offer a few examples for you to consider here. These are just suggestions. You can act individually or as a group. If you find that one of them touches you, by all means use it, but you may also think of other individual or group actions that inspire you.

In 1792, Bishop John Carroll invoked the blessing of the mother of God upon the newly formed United States and placed the nation under her patronage. In 1846, the Holy See formalized this designation for the American bishops. Since that time, devotion to the mother of God has had a significant place in Catholic life in our country. Take a virtual tour of the Basilica of the National Shrine of the Immaculate Conception in Washington, D.C. (www. nationalshrine.com) to experience the art and architecture of what is called "America's Catholic Church."

The great devotional prayer to the Blessed Mother is the rosary, a practice that dates back to the Middle Ages. This week, review the sacred mysteries of the rosary. Pray the rosary alone or with others this week. Ask Mary to help you be a more mature disciple of Christ.

Can you think of people who have given the type of witness and discipleship that is demonstrated in the pondering of Mary? Read about the Mothers of the Plaza de Mayo in Buenos Aires, Argentina. What is needed for the kind of peaceful witness they embody? Take your witness to the public square. Ask others to be a part of witnessing with you—for example, protesting an unjust policy or decision.

Closing Prayer

Share together prayers of intercession or praise.

Then pray this closing prayer together:

> Loving God,
> our mother Mary did not hesitate to do your will.
> In the magnitude of her discipleship
> we see the way of holiness revealed.
> We call out to you by her intercession
> to be relieved of anything
>   that would separate us from you.
> Help the Church to become
>   of one heart and one mind
> in Christ's name we pray.
> Amen.

or

The Memorare

Remember, O most gracious Virgin Mary,
that never was it known that anyone who fled

to your protection,
implored your help, or sought your intercession,
was left unaided.
Inspired with this confidence,
I fly to you, O Virgin of virgins, my Mother;
to you do I come, before you I stand,
sinful and sorrowful.
O Mother of the Word Incarnate,
despise not my petitions,
but in your mercy hear and answer me.
Amen.

Looking Ahead

Prepare for your next session by prayerfully reading and studying Session 11. You can also supplement your preparation by reading Sacred Fire, *pages 166 to 210.*

Informal Gathering

Drawing Strength from Prayer

Essential Kinds of Prayer

Sharing

Briefly share on one of the following questions:

"How am I right now?" or
"What good news would I like to share?"

Sharing the Good News

Share how you did with your action response from the last session (Living the Good News) or how you were able to incorporate the message of the last session into your daily life.

Lifting Our Hearts

... in Song

Play or sing the following song or another song of your choosing:

"Here I Am Lord"

... in the Quiet

Pause for a few moments of silence, and allow yourself to more deeply embrace the presence of God.

... in the Word

Read aloud Luke 11:1-13

As the reader proclaims the sacred text, allow yourself to ponder a word, a phrase, a question, or a feeling that rises up from within you. Reflect on this in silence; when you are invited, briefly share it aloud with our group.

(If no one wishes to speak, simply allow the group to be enveloped in the silence, and allow the reflection to continue for a few more moments.)

... in Prayer

> Heavenly Father,
> with unending patience,
> you wait for your children
> to turn their hearts and minds to you.
> Like a loving parent
> who aches to hear
> the successes and heartbreaks,
> the challenges and victories
> of her daughters and sons.
> you long for us to bring ourselves to you,
> heart, mind, and soul.
> Help us to remember that your door will open
> if only we would knock.
> Help us to seek you in every place,
> confident that we will find you.
> In the name of Christ Jesus, we pray.
> Amen.

Our Companion on the Journey

Thomas Merton

"Prayer does not blind us to the world, but it transforms
our vision of the world, and makes us see it, all men,
and all the history of mankind, in the light of God.
To pray 'in spirit and in truth' enables us to enter into
contact with that infinite love, that inscrutable freedom which is at work behind the complexities and the
intricacies of human existence. This does not mean fab-
ricating for ourselves pious rationalizations to explain
everything that happens. It involves no surreptitious
manipulation of the hard truths of life."

Thomas Merton, *Contemplative Prayer*

THOMAS MERTON WAS A TRAPPIST MONK who
first attracted attention with *The Seven Storey
Mountain*, an autobiography describing his search
for God. Merton wrote sixty other books as well as
hundreds of articles, poems, and prayers on topics
including pacifism and spirituality. Deeply affected
by World War II and the momentous social change
it set in motion, he sought answers spiritually and
intellectually.

Merton was born in France. His mother died
when he was six, and over the next decade his
father, a painter, either left the boy with relatives
or took him along to a variety of locales. Thomas
attended private residential schools in France
and England and, at 18, entered Clare College at
Cambridge. In his autobiography he describes an

undisciplined youth in which he drank to excess. He was also known to be sexually promiscuous and financially irresponsible. His attitude toward religion during his early life ranged from indifference, to fitful interest, to avowed agnosticism.

After a year, Merton left Cambridge, moved to his grandparent's home in Douglaston, N.Y., and began commuting to Columbia University in Manhattan. After graduation from Columbia, Merton began an intellectual and spiritual personal journey. He began attending Mass regularly and found solace and peace in the liturgy of the Church. After reading a description of the conversion of Gerard Manly Hopkins, Merton came to believe he was called to a similar path. He converted to Catholicism and began an even more intense study of the tradition.

In 1942 Merton joined the Abbey of Gethsemane in Kentucky, a community of the Order of Cistercians of the Strict Observance (commonly called the Trappists). He was ordained a priest in 1949. He spent 27 years as a member of the community, following its ascetic monastic rule and observance of silence while living in the abbey and also alone in a hermitage.

In the late 1950s and early 1960s, Merton became more and more concerned with social justice issues, including racial inequality, the arms race, and the war in Vietnam. He began writing prolifically on war and peace. In 1962, after the publication of his "Cold War Letters," Merton's superiors forbade him to continue writing about war, telling him to focus exclusively on peace.

Merton believed that the Christian mystical tradition had been neglected, and his books brought forward practices of prayer and meditation that had been long lost to mainstream Christians. For Merton, the path of silence was the key to living in peace despite the inner contradictions of human life.

In his last years, Merton became very interested in dialogue with Asian religions and was instrumental in promoting a monastic dialogue with Zen Buddhists. While at an interfaith conference in Bangkok, he was accidentally electrocuted by a malfunctioning fan as he stepped out of his bath. He was 53.

Encountering Wisdom for Life

THE LIFE OF THE MATURE DISCIPLE is, in fact, busy or full, depending on a few critical factors. Rich in demands, including the responsibilities of child rearing, career building, and caring for elders, adult life is—in the words of Fr. Rolheiser—more of a marathon than a sprint. Too often, exhaustion and pressure wear down both the will and the ability to live as a mature disciple. Without God's help, it can feel like too much for us.

We know from the Gospels that in his humanity even Jesus was not immune to needing his Father's help. We see him in the desert, adrift in the Sea of Galilee, and on the mountaintop taking a break from the demands of his ministry. And we see him in constant prayer: "He prays when he is joy-filled; he prays when he is in agony; he prays with others around him; he prays when he is alone at night," observes Fr. Rolheiser. Jesus' constant connection with the Father inspires his disciples, who ask him to teach them to pray.

Although the *Baltimore Catechism* has been retired, it contains a simple sentence that captures the essence of what prayer is: Prayer is the lifting of our hearts and minds to God. In this experience, we are invited to give to God whatever it is that we carry in that moment. We can lift our joy and gratitude. We can also lift our boredom, our skepticism, our exhaustion, or our obsessions.

How often should we do that? St. Paul said that we should pray "without ceasing" (1 Thessalonians 5:17). This does not mean we are to head to a hermitage to sit in silent prayer 24/7. Rather, it means moving between moments of formal prayer and moments in which we are living our lives against what Fr. Rolheiser calls "a certain horizon"—an awareness of God. Just as a woman heads out to a corporate meeting, laptop in hand, but still holds in her consciousness thoughts of her spouse and children, we can be out in life aware of God, in whom we "live and move and have our being" (Acts 17:28).

Prayer takes many forms. Some of our prayer is private, and some is public, such as attending Mass or praying *The Liturgy of the Hours* with others. Fr. Rolheiser suggests new names—"priestly" and "affective"— in hope of providing us with a fresh entry point for our practice of prayer.

"Priestly prayer is the prayer of Christ through the Church for the world," explains Fr. Rolheiser. We offer priestly prayer whenever we act on behalf of others rather than in our own self-interest. We also pray priestly prayer whenever we pray the prayer of the Church in the Eucharist or *The Liturgy of the Hours*. We pray these prayers as mature members of the Body of Christ, no longer solitary and individual, but joined with the universal Church and with Christ in praying for all of creation.

Affective prayer, Fr. Rolheiser's second category, is designed to draw us into a deeper personal relationship with God. Affective prayer includes praying the rosary, meditation, centering prayer, spontaneous devotions, and other forms of non-liturgical prayer.

Affective prayer can open us in a deep way to a simple and powerful reality: the love of God. Affective prayer allows us to hear the God, who has called us by name, respond to our prayer with a depth of affection almost beyond our capacity to comprehend. We also make prayers of petition. We can pray for guidance from God. We can present our fears and insecurities to God—a sign of the depth of love and trust we place in him. The challenges associated with this type of prayer are first, to offer it in total candor and humility ("I'm afraid!" "I'm filled with anger and confusion!") and second, to "wait upon the Lord" for direction. Often we are desperate for a response from God, and it feels almost impossible to wait and discern God's direction.

Finally, there is a long tradition in Christianity of praying for the dead. We do this because we believe in the resurrection and the Communion of Saints. All of those who live in Christ die in Christ and are raised to new life in him. Praying for those who have died, both those we have known and people we have never met, not only does us good, providing solace in seasons of grief, but it also connects us to them. In this prayer we can find healing and forgiveness, comfort and connection. And we believe our prayer is comfort and connection for them as well. The mature disciple must sustain himself or herself in prayer by creating space for an interior life. It is easy to say, "I'm too busy, too stressed, too tired, or too preoccupied to sit or kneel down and pray." We have to make an effort to make prayer a priority.

Equally challenging can be the restlessness that overcomes us as we try to pray. This "congenital disquiet" is an uneasiness that the culture likes to fan into even higher flame. Listen to this song! Watch this movie! Buy this new device! Take this vacation! We are constantly prodded to crave experience, which can become an impediment to the silent letting go that prayer asks of us.

Added to that is the fundamental "ambiguity" of prayer. First, it isn't easy: It requires commitment and practice. Second, it's far from pragmatic: On the surface, it appears as if we are doing nothing. And third, it does not provide the immediate, instant response we are conditioned to expect. Prayer might not immediately alleviate our headaches or heartaches.

The good news, however, is that if we pray—sometimes filled with the awareness of God's life in and love for us, sometimes dry as a bone and filled with emptiness—we will build our relationship. Over time, our faithfulness to the relationship with God, exemplified by our prayer life, becomes deep and intimate. However we choose to pray, our prayers will support our actions as the followers of Jesus, and help us be more effective in participating in bringing the kingdom of God into its fullness for all.

✛ ✛ ✛

Sharing Our Faith

✛ Which are you more comfortable with: Priestly prayer or affective prayer? Why? What would you have to do to achieve a balance between the two? Do you find yourself resisting one or the other? Why? What do you pray for?

✛ Can you identify obstacles that impede your ability to have a full prayer life? What are they? Which obstacle are you willing to take action to remove?

✛ Fr. Rolheiser asserts that "purgatory is not a geographic place distinct from heaven but the pain that comes from being in heaven without having fully let go of earth." What is your reaction to this definition? How are you consciously aware of the Communion of Saints? Do you pray for the dead?

Living the Good News

Where do you find yourself stirred by the Word of God and his presence among and within your group? What action might you take in response to this? Share with your group what you will do, within the context of your own life, to act upon what you have experienced.

We offer a few examples for you to consider here. These are just suggestions. You can act individually or as a group. If you find that one of them touches you, by all means use it, but you may also think of other individual or group actions that inspire you.

- Make time this week for meditation. Use a practice like Centering Prayer (find a description at www.centeringprayer.com, or in books by Fr. Basil Pennington or Fr. Thomas Keating) or the Jesus Prayer (in which you repeat, "Lord Jesus Christ, Son of God, have mercy on me, the sinner") to open your heart and mind to God's presence. Do you find meditation easy? Difficult? Write in your journal about your experience. This week, meditate before you take an action of service, and notice in what ways meditation impacts your experience.

- Do the groups in which you serve at the parish or in other settings include prayer in their gatherings? Offer to be a prayer leader or to prepare prayer for an activity in which prayer is not usually included. Pray for God's guidance as you begin a meeting, either silently or aloud. Incorporate prayer into your commute or any activity that starts your day. Close your day with reflection and prayers of gratitude.

- Each day, read the closing prayer in this session by Thomas Merton. Why do you think this prayer speaks to so many people? Visit with someone that you believe is very prayerful. Ask that person to share with you about his or her prayer life. Consider crafting a personal prayer to God, like Merton's. If you are comfortable, share it with someone you love or members of your group. Where does your prayer lead you?

Closing Prayer

Share together prayers of intercession or praise.

Then pray together this closing prayer by Thomas Merton:

> My Lord God, I have no idea where I am going.
> I do not see the road ahead of me.
> I cannot know for certain where it will end.
> Nor do I really know myself,
> and the fact that I think I am following your will
> does not mean that I am actually doing so.
> But I believe that the desire to please you
> does, in fact, please you.
> And I hope I have that desire in all that I am doing.
> I hope that I will never do anything
> apart from that desire.
> And I know that if I do this
> you will lead me by the right road,
> though I may know nothing about it.
> Therefore, I will trust you always
> though I may seem to be lost
> and in the shadow of death.
> I will not fear, for you are ever with me,
> and you will never leave me to face my perils alone.
> Amen.

Looking Ahead

Prepare for your next session by prayerfully reading and studying Session 12. You can also supplement your preparation by reading Sacred Fire, *pages 210 to 242.*

Informal Gathering

The Crowning Glory of Discipleship

To Bless and Be a Blessing

Sharing

Briefly share on one of the following questions:

"How am I right now?" or
"What good news would I like to share?"

Sharing the Good News

Share how you did with your action response from the last session (Living the Good News) or how you were able to incorporate the message of the last session into your daily life.

Lifting Our Hearts

... in Song

Play or sing one the following song or another song of your choosing:

"This Is (Song of Micah)"

... in the Quiet

Pause for a few moments of silence, and allow yourself to more deeply embrace the presence of God.

... in the Word

Read aloud Matthew 5:2-12

As the reader proclaims the sacred text, allow yourself to ponder a word, a phrase, a question, or a feeling that rises up from within you. Reflect on this in silence; when you are invited, briefly share it aloud with our group.

(If no one wishes to speak, simply allow the group to be enveloped in the silence, and allow the reflection to continue for a few more moments.)

... in Prayer

God our Father
you set in motion the wondrous creation
and seeing it, you named it "very good."
Forgive us for the times we have not cherished this gift.
Forgive us for when we have not cherished one another
as you cherish each one of us.
Empower us with the ability to see you
in all places and all things.
For we are truly blessed
to be your children and to know your love.
In the name of Jesus, we pray.
Amen.

Our Companion on the Journey

St. Benedict of Nursia

"At the gate of the monastery
let there be placed a wise old man,
who knows how to receive and to give a message,
and whose maturity will prevent him from straying about.
This porter should have a room near the gate,

so that those who come may always find someone at hand
to attend to their business.
And as soon as anyone knocks or a poor person hails him,
let him answer 'Thanks be to God' or 'A blessing!'
Then let him attend to them promptly,
with all the meekness inspired by the fear of God
and with the warmth of charity."

The Rule of Benedict

S T. BENEDICT OF NURSIA was the son of a Roman
nobleman in a mountain village northeast
of Rome. Tradition places Benedict's birth in the
year 480. An account of his life, written by Pope
Gregory I, describes a young man who abandoned
his classical studies in rhetoric because he found
life in Rome too decadent. According to Gregory,
Benedict feared for his soul and, forsaking his
inheritance, fled to the town of Subiaco, where he
lived for three years as a hermit under the direction of another monk, Romanus.

Eventually, Benedict began establishing monasteries, each with 12 monks, in the region south
of Rome. Around the year 529, he traveled to
Monte Cassino. Destroying the pagan Temple of
Apollo that had stood there for centuries, he and
his brother monks built a monastery on its foot-
print. This community became the heart of his
monastic system. St. Scholastica, his twin sister,
followed Benedict into monastic life, establishing
a monastery for women five miles from Monte
Cassino.

Benedict wrote a practical treatise on living a
holy life, the *Rule of St. Benedict*, which guided the

lives of the monasteries he founded. The 73 short chapters reveal a deep comprehension of human nature as well as a clear sense of the actions required of committed disciples. His innovation of praying the *Divine Office* placed a liturgical heart in the body of the monasticism that he formed, and the practices of *lectio divina* (slowly reading and reflecting on Scripture) and contemplation provided clear paths for knowing Christ more fully. For prayer, Benedict instructed the brothers to turn to the psalms, the ancient and sacred songs of the Jews that shaped the life of Jesus himself. The rule offers guidelines for such things as decision-making, leadership, silence, fraternal correction, care of the vessels of the altar, garments, maintenance of the kitchen, sleeping, travelling, and working in the fields.

Hospitality is one of the hallmarks of the rule, thus the practice by the porter of the monastery of blessing each person who comes to the monastery door. Among the most famous lines of the rule is the beautiful instruction that "All guests who present themselves are to be welcomed as Christ, for he himself will say: I was a stranger and you welcomed me (Matthew 25:35)."

The Rule of St. Benedict is still followed by male and female Benedictine, Trappist, and Cistercian monastic communities around the world. Its precepts are also practiced by lay people who are oblates—that is, men and women who are associated with a monastery without living in the religious community or taking vows.

Countless Christians have been drawn to the

spirituality of the rule, which emphasizes right relationships and seeing the divine life in the ordinary.

Benedict reportedly died standing in prayer with his brothers in the oratory of the monastery.

Encountering Wisdom for Life

IN TODAY'S WORLD, IT IS COMMONPLACE to hear the words "God bless you!" when someone sneezes. This is usually said lightly, often no more than a toss-away cordial expression. The origin of the practice is lost in antiquity, but in the late sixth century, Pope Gregory the Great urged constant prayer during an epidemic of bubonic plague; he specifically directed that anyone who sneezed be immediately blessed, because sneezing was considered a first sign that a person had contracted the illness. By the middle of the eighth century, it was common for someone to say "God bless you" in response to a sneeze.

We may say those words today without thinking, but in fact a blessing is one of the most powerful gifts that a mature disciple can give, observes Fr. Rolheiser. It is a practice that all of us could—and should—take much more seriously.

The word "blessing" is derived from the Latin word *benedicere*, which means "to speak well of." The Old Testament is filled with stories of blessing. The Book of Genesis says that on each of the first six days of creation God offered his blessing on what had been accomplished, observing that it "was good." We hear the voice of God in the New Testament, as well, when Jesus is baptized by John in the Jordan River: "You are my beloved Son; with you I am well pleased" (Luke 3:22).

Like his Father, Jesus offers the people, and us, his blessing. The people hear Jesus tell them that even in the midst of hardship, loss, and grief, they are blessed—in fact, they, the least, are the beloved of God, the ones in whom God delights. For thousands of years, the words of Jesus in the beatitudes (Matthew 5:1-10, Luke 6:20-23) have comforted and challenged his followers.

It is because of his awareness of the depth of his own blessing, his "blessed consciousness," that Jesus can see all the world as blessed. Thomas Aquinas explored what it means to have our human perceptions colored by our interior reality, and he applied it to his sacramental theology. Thomas's declaration, "whatever is received is received according to the manner of the one receiving," means that our consciousness either opens us to the grace of God or impedes the flow of God's grace.

We live in a world in which many people have never had the experience of being blessed, and because of that, they are unable to be people of blessing in return. Their experience is the polar opposite of blessing; they have experienced being cursed. To curse is not simply to sling ugly, socially unacceptable vocabulary at another. Fr. Rolheiser writes that every act of suppression, diminishment, or abuse of power is, in effect, a curse. It is a curse to think "You are an idiot" or to turn to someone in his or her vulnerability and say "Who do you think you are?" Whenever we suppress or shame another, whenever we are unforgiving judges, we are cursing. Whenever we gossip or bad mouth someone, we are cursing that person. Whenever we demean people or withhold affirmation, we are cursing them.

If, over time, we are cursed more than we are blessed, there are significant consequences. Fr. Rolheiser points to the epidemic of depression in this era and suggests that it is, in part, a byproduct of insufficient blessing of one another. Our inability to experience delight and joy—something often seen only in young children—reflects the barren state of people who are cursed.

How do we turn this tide? What is involved in becoming people of blessing?

A blessing has three components. The first is seeing. "To really see someone, especially a younger person who looks up to you, is to give that person a blessing," writes Fr. Rolheiser. Whether at a pool, in the backyard, or in a park, most parents have experienced their children asking, ad nauseam, "Watch me!" When the loving parent casts her gaze on the 57th cannonball splash, she is blessing that child: "You are delightful!" her gaze says. "You are unique and special, talented and entertaining, and you are loved!" The blessing of seeing people is available throughout our lives, in examples such as those above and in formal experiences and rituals such as meeting a public or religious figure. It plays out on sports fields, in corporate settings and more: "We are blessed by being seen, and we bless others by seeing them," notes Fr. Rolheiser.

Second, blessing is spoken. When we take the time to sincerely say something positive—"I'm glad you're here! You are valued!"—we imitate God the Father at the baptism of Jesus. In our ministries, families, and business settings, we bless others when we affirm them for who they are or when we express our deep appreciation for being part of their lives.

How often do we feel the urge to acknowledge and appreciate people, but somehow also feel hesitant or impeded? Being

persons of blessing demands that we push through to a place of greater courage and generosity.

Finally, blessing involves what St. Francis calls "self-forgetting." When we are willing to give up something so that someone else might have more, we have experienced the third aspect of blessing. The story of the magi reveals the power of this life-giving blessing. Unlike Herod, who in his fear curses the birth of the newborn king and seeks his destruction, the magi place gifts at the baby's feet. Then, they disappear. They have given to the new young king and have slipped into anonymity, their task complete.

Parenting well demands this same sort of self-gift. To raise healthy and whole children requires sacrifice. So, too, does great mentoring and good pastoring. But when we are stingy or grasping, or not willing to create a place for those who come in our wake, we curse others.

Taking on the practice of blessing is an act of mature discipleship. God blesses the world, and then we are the channel in which that blessing flows to others. Fr. Rolheiser observes that blessings are particularly powerful when they are offered within the same gender: Mother to daughter, father to son, elder to protégé. This is true simply because we are less threatened in our status and power by those of a different gender.

We might think that the "crowning glory" of discipleship is martyrdom—dying for another. Jesus himself describes this as the greatest love we can offer. But Fr. Rolheiser writes that we were not born for martyrdom but for "eternal Sabbath." "The final picture rather is that of a blessing grandmother or a blessing grandfather, not suffering but joyful, smiling and beaming with pride at the life and energy of the young, basking in that energy and radiating from every power of his or her being the words of the Creator: 'It is good! Indeed, it is very good! In you I take delight!'"

✠ ✠ ✠

Sharing Our Faith

✠ Think about your spiritual life. When has someone blessed
you? Where were you? What words were said? Was it a
"formal" blessing of the Church or something spontaneous
offered to you in the midst of life? How did it feel to be the
object of someone's blessing?

✠ Have you ever given someone a blessing? Where and when?
If you have never given someone a blessing, why not?

✠ "The mark of a deeply mature man or woman, the mark of a
very mature disciple of Jesus, and the mark of someone truly
giving his or her life away is this: he or she is a person who
blesses others and blesses the world, just as God does and just
as Jesus did." What is implied here? Why do you think Fr.
Rolheiser considers blessing the "crowning glory of discipleship, beyond martyrdom"? Do you agree with him? Why or
why not?

Living the Good News

*Where do you find yourself stirred by the Word of God and his pres-
ence among and within your group? What action might you take in
response to this? Share with your group what you will do, within
the context of your own life, to act upon what you have experienced.*

*We offer a few examples for you to consider here. These are just sug-
gestions. You can act individually or as a group. If you find that one
of them touches you, by all means use it, but you may also think of
other individual or group actions that inspire you.*

🌐 Begin a practice of blessing others. This could be saying "God Bless you" to a loved one at a time other than

a sneeze. You could say this as you end a phone call, for example. If you have young children in your life, you could draw the sign of the cross on their foreheads at bedtime or as they depart for school and say, "God bless you." Your blessing could be words of appreciation or acknowledgement. As you do this, note how people react to your blessings.

Fr. Rolheiser observes "that hunger for the father's blessing is one of the deepest hungers in the whole world, especially among men." Is there anyone from whom you are withholding your blessing? If there is, what might you do to change that?

In what ways and with what phrases do people today curse each other? This week, listen for this phenomenon. See if you can identify curses you hear in the world. Watch for those that are obvious and those that are more insidious. Pay attention to your personal interactions and notice if there are moments in which you are cursing others. Think of one place you could impact and shift cursing to blessing, and act on it. Develop the habit of blessing others.

How open are you to the final blessing in Mass? This week, pray that you will receive its power and grace in a new way.

✠ ✠ ✠

Closing Prayer

Share together prayers of intercession or praise.

Then pray together this closing prayer:

> "Speak to Aaron and his sons and tell them: This is how
>   you shall bless the Israelites.
> Say to them:
> The LORD bless you and keep you!
> The LORD let his face shine upon you, and be gracious
>   to you!
> The LORD look upon you kindly and give you peace!"*
> Lord, bless us in the days ahead
> and make us people of blessing,
> a source of your kindness and peace
> in every place we are found.
> Amen.
>
> *Numbers 6:23-26

Informal Gathering

Looking Back, Looking Ahead ...

Looking Back ...

- Reflecting on your experience with Living in the Sacred, share as a group:
    1. What has touched your heart?
    2. What experiences have helped you grow as a person and as a community? Why?
    3. How has faith sharing moved you to live out the Gospel in a new way?
- What acts of welcome, charity, or justice by your group were inspired by your faith sharing. Send your Good News stories and pictures to goodnews@renewintl.org

Looking Ahead ...

Stay connected

- Pray for and stay in touch with each other.
- Encourage one another to participate in parish outreach efforts.
- Read our inspirational reflections at blog.renewintl.org
- "Like" us at Facebook.com/renewintl
- Subscribe to the *World RENEW* enewsletter at www.renewintl.org/subscribe

Keep it going

- Continue to faith share all year round. See RENEW International's resources on pages 147-156.
- View and discuss Turning Points: Witness Stories, a RENEW video series at youtube.com/user/turningpointsstories
- Share your Living in the Sacred experience with family, friends, and fellow parishioners. Encourage others to experience faith-sharing in a small group.

Music Appendix

Songs are listed by title, author and/or composer, copyright holder or publisher; also indicated is an album on which the song appears.

These songs are on RENEW International's CD *Songs for Longing for the Holy.* You can get more information and/or order this CD online at www.renewintl.org/spirtualityCD.

SESSION 1
"Weave One Heart"
Marty Haugen (GIA)
Spirit of Malia

SESSION 2
"Everyday God"
Bernadette Farrell (OCP)
Restless is the Heart

SESSION 3
"For Living, for Dying"
Donna Peña (GIA)
Spirit of Malia

SESSION 4
"Heal Me, Lord"
Cathy Riso (Olive Branch
   Publishing/Frankie's Farm
   Music)
*Renew the Face of the Earth,
   Volume II*

SESSION 5
"Gathered in the Love of
   Christ"
Marty Haugen (GIA)
The Song and the Silence

SESSION 6
"Anthem: We Are Called, We
   Are Chosen"
Tom Conry (OCP)
Consecrated

SESSION 7
"River of Glory"
Daniel L. Schutte (OCP)
*Glory in the Cross-Music for the
   Easter Triduum*

SESSION 8
"We Come to Your Feast"
Michael Joncas (GIA)
Spirit of Malia

SESSION 9
"I Am for You"
Rory Cooney (GIA)
Spirit of Malia

SESSION 10
"We Have Been Told"
David Haas (GIA)
*You Are Mine: The Best of
   David Haas, Volume 2*

SESSION 11
"Here I Am, Lord"
Michael Ward (WLP)
Sing My Soul

SESSION 12
"This Is (Song of Micah)"
Liam Lawton (GIA)
In the Quiet

Addresses of Publishers of Music Resources

GIA Publications, Inc.
7404 South Mason Avenue
Chicago, IL 60638
Phone: 800-442-1358 *or* 708-496-3800
Website: www.giamusic.com
Email: custserv@giamusic.com

Oregon Catholic Press
(OCP) Publications
5526 NE Hassalo
Portland, OR 97213
Phone: 800-548-8749
Website: www.ocp.org
Email: liturgy@ocp.org

White Dove Productions, Inc.
Phone: 406-624-6151
Website: www.whitedoveproductions.com
Email: info@whitedoveproductions.com
Permissions processed by www.musicservices.com

World Library Publications
3708 River Road
Suite 400
Franklin Park, IL 60131
Phone: 800-621-5197
Website: www.wlpmusic.com
Email: wlpcs@jspaluch.com

Acknowledgments

WE GRATEFULLY ACKNOWLEDGE the use of the following quotations:

The scripture quotations contained herein are from the New Revised Standard Version Bible (containing the Old and New Testaments with the Apocryphal/Deuterocanonical Books), copyright © 1989 by the Division of Christian Education of the National Council of the Churches of Christ in the U.S.A., and are used by permission. All rights reserved.

Reasonable effort has been made to locate original sources. When not available, secondary sources are included. Where citations are not included, quotations are considered to be fair use of copyrighted work. The publisher appreciates information on original sources and will include them in subsequent printings.

pp. 16-17, from *The Collected Works of St. John of the Cross*, translated by Kieran Kavanaugh and Otilio Rodriguez. Copyright © 1964, 1979, 1991 by Washington Province of Discalced Carmelites, ICS Publications, 2131 Lincoln Road, N.E. Washington, DC 20002-1199; www.icspublications.org. Used with permission.

pp. 28-29, "Martha and Mary" from *John Newton's Olney Hymns*. © Curiosmith, PO Box 390293, Minneapolis, MN 55439. www.curiosmith.com; email: shopkeeper@curiosmith.com. Used with permission.

p. 41, from Pope Francis, Angelus address, August 24, 2014, http://w2.vatican.va/content/francesco/en/angelus/2014/documents/papa-francesco_angelus_20140824.html.

ACKNOWLEDGEMENTS

p. 51, from Dietrich Bonhoeffer, Life Together: *The Classic Exploration of Faith in Community*, © 1954 Harper & Row Publishers, www.harpercollins.com.

pp. 60-61, from *The Hidden Life* by Edith Stein. © 1992 Washington Province of Discalced Carmelites, ICS Publications, 2131 Lincoln Road, N.E., Washington, DC 20002-1199; www.icspublications.org. Used with permission.

p. 62, from Edith Stein's letter to Pope Pius XI, www.baltimorecarmel.org/saints/Stein/letter%20to%20pope.htm.

p. 71, from *The Wounded Healer* by Henri Nouwen. © Henri Nouwen. An Image Book, published by Doubleday, NY, NY.

p. 81, from Pope St. John XXIII, Address at the opening of the Second Vatican Council, October 11, 1962; http://www.thedivinemercy.org/library/article.php?NID=5666.

p. 91, from St Thérèse of Lisieux in a letter to her cousin, Marie Guerin in *Thoughts of the Servant of God Therese of the Child Jesus*, P.J. Kennedy and Sons, New York, NY; 1915.

p. 123, from Thomas Merton, *Contemplative Prayer.* ©1969 The Merton Legacy Trust. Image Books ©1996 Crown Publishing, a division of Random House www.crownpublishing.com.

pp. 132-133, from "On Porters of the Monastery," The Rule of Benedict, Chapter 66.

Resources from RENEW International

LONGING FOR THE HOLY: Spirituality for Everyday Life
Based on selected insights of Ronald Rolheiser, OMI

Experience how the gentle spiritual guidance and practical
wisdom of best-selling Catholic author Fr. Ronald Rolheiser,
OMI, can enliven everyday life. Suitable for small-community
faith sharing or individual reflection, *Longing for the Holy* covers

different dimensions of contemporary
spiritual life for those who want to
enrich their sense of the presence of God
and develop a deeper spirituality.

The Participant's Book contains
twelve sessions with prayers, reflections,
sharing questions, and stories from
saints and contemporary people of faith.

The songs suggested for the moments of prayer in
the faith-sharing sessions are offered on the
13-song music CD.

Luke: My Spirit Rejoices!

Written by scripture scholar Martin
Lang, *Luke: My Spirit Rejoices!* engages
readers with the entire Gospel and
includes reflections on the content
of the Gospel, the human behavior
illuminated in Luke's work, and
the Old Testament background for
each passage. Sharing questions and
opportunities to apply the gospel
message to daily life make this a perfect resource for small
Christian communities. Can be used individually or in a group.

Creation at the Crossroads

A Small-Group Resource on Pope Francis' *"On Care for Our Common Home (Laudato Si')"*

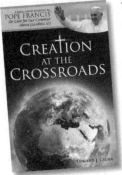

With twelve sessions on Pope Francis' encyclical on ecology, *On Care for Our Common Home (Laudato Si')*, this resource is designed for use in parishes, small groups, and college campus ministries. Through Scripture, prayer, reflections, faith-sharing questions, and practical ideas for protecting and caring for the environment and people, this resource will move Catholics—small groups and their members—to faith-based action.

At Prayer with Mary

At Prayer with Mary offers seven sessions on the life and mystery of Mary that will deepen your appreciation of and devotion to our Blessed Mother Mary and enrich your prayer experiences. Over the centuries, Mary's example has inspired Christians to imitate her by saying "yes" to God's call in their own lives. Her faithfulness, as it is portrayed in the Gospel narratives, is a model of the prayerful kind of life Jesus calls us to. Scripture, Catholic teaching, personal testimonies, and Marian prayer—including the rosary—provide a renewed appreciation of Mary's place in today's world, where she, as always, points the way to Christ.

ALSO AN
e
BOOK

Also available as an **eBook**!

A **14-song CD** is also available and contains the songs suggested for use during the moments of prayer.

Advent Awakenings

Advent is a time of spiritual anticipation amidst the often distracting preparations for Christmas. Stay focused on the significance of this season with *Advent Awakenings*, a four-session faith-sharing experience grounded in the Sunday gospel readings.

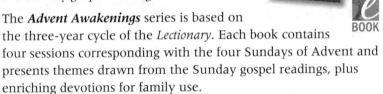

ALSO AN

e

BOOK

The *Advent Awakenings* series is based on the three-year cycle of the *Lectionary*. Each book contains four sessions corresponding with the four Sundays of Advent and presents themes drawn from the Sunday gospel readings, plus enriching devotions for family use.

Appropriate for seasonal groups, small Christian communities, and individual reflection and prayer.

Also available as an **eBook**!

A **15-song CD** contains the songs suggested for use during the prayerful reflections of each faith-sharing session for years A, B, and C.

Lenten Longings

Make a six-week retreat by exploring the Sunday readings of Lent. Based on the three-year cycle of the *Lectionary*, each book contains six sessions corresponding to the six weeks of Lent and presents themes drawn from the year's Lenten readings. Simple language and everyday metaphors steep you in the season's promptings to surrender self, work for justice, and deepen prayer life.

ALSO AN

e

BOOK

Lenten Longings is well suited for seasonal groups, small Christian communities, and individual reflection.

Also available as an **eBook!**

An **18-song CD** contains the songs suggested for use during the prayerful reflections of each faith-sharing session for years A, B, and C.

PrayerTime: Faith-Sharing Reflections on the Sunday Gospels

This faith-sharing resource responds to the U.S. Bishops' suggestion that "every parish meeting can begin with the reading of the upcoming Sunday's Gospel, followed by a time of reflection and faith sharing."

With each Sunday's Gospel as a focus, **PrayerTime** proposes meaningful reflections, focused faith-sharing questions, related questions for consideration, and prayers as a source of spiritual nourishment and inspiration.

Use **PrayerTime** any time of year, whenever the small community needs. It is also ideal for beginning meetings of the pastoral council, staff, and other parish groups. The themes can also be read personally as a way to prepare for Sunday Mass.

GLEANINGS: A Personal Prayer Journal

Many participants in small communities tell us how much they are helped in both their shared discussion and their personal reflection by the technique known as journaling: keeping a notebook for the expression of thoughts and ideas.

Gleanings is a valuable tool for both avid and occasional journal writers. Each page spread is decorated with a spiritual quotation or musing that can inspire prayerful reflection on your relationship with God. The comfortably-sized format makes it an excellent companion for your personal faith journey, helping tap into the richness of God's wisdom within you. It is also a thoughtful gift for friends or family.

Small-Group Leader Series

SOWING SEEDS
Essentials for Small Community Leaders

This book offers a comprehensive collection of pastoral insights and practical suggestions to help small-community leaders guide their groups in a way that nourishes spiritual growth. Culled from RENEW International's three decades of experience in pioneering and promoting small Christian communities, this book overflows with simple but effective ideas and strategies that will enhance the way these groups reflect on and respond to the Gospel.

Also available as an **eBook**!

Leading Prayer in Small Groups

Have you ever been asked to lead prayer for your church group, council, or committee? *Leading Prayer in Small Groups* encourages you in leading fruitful group prayer experiences with confidence. *Leading Prayer in Small Groups* emphasizes the importance of group prayer for church groups of every kind and provides insight into why we pray. It also explains the role, qualities, and duties of a leader of prayer. Readers are guided through the stages of preparing group prayer and the process of effectively leading prayer for a group.

Scenes from a Parish

Special Edition DVD and Film Faith-Sharing Guides
In English and Spanish

Get a rare glimpse into one parish's real-world experience as it struggles to reconcile ideals of faith with the realities of today's changing and diverse culture.

View, reflect upon, and share faith with this special edition film and *Faith-Sharing Guide* and its important themes of welcoming the stranger, offering compassion, and feeding the hungry.

Ideal for parish-wide, small-group, and personal viewing and reflection.

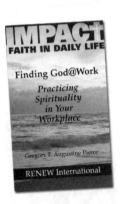

Finding God@Work

Six faith-sharing sessions guide us on a quest: can God be found at work? If so, how? Examine your lived experience of work—both positively and negatively—from a spiritual vantage point, considering relevant passages from Scripture, and principles of Catholic social teaching.

Forgiveness and Reconciliation

The insightful wisdom and many inspiring stories of forgiveness and reconciliation offer a profound understanding of people's desire to be forgiven and the steps to take to live reconciled lives. Reflect on the healing power of God and the richness of the sacrament of reconciliation to discover again how to live in the freedom of God.

Be My Witness

Be My Witness is a two-year, a Christ-centered, Spirit-led process to transform parishes and form disciples for the New Evangelization. The New Evangelization represents a special responsibility for leaders in the Church—helping baptized Catholics embrace their role in passing on the flame of faith and setting hearts on fire to bring Christ's warmth and light to all.

Based on Pope Francis' landmark document on evangelization, *The Joy of the Gospel*, *Be My Witness* engages parish staff, lay leaders, and parishioners to form them to be committed disciples of Christ. Print and digital resources and interactive training videos form and fire up a Spirit-led team to reach out to the uninvolved, unchurched, and marginalized in your parish and community.

Also included in *Be My Witness* is the RENEW Parish Assessment. This assessment assists pastors, staff, and key leaders in affirming areas of strength, identifying areas of opportunity, and strategically planning for full and active participation in the mission of the New Evangelization.

The process contains a faith stories video series that presents witness stories for the New Evangelization. These videos show everyday Catholics who came to know Christ and grew in faith through the words and actions of friends, family, priests, and others along the way. By watching and reflecting on these videos, participants are encouraged to become joy-filled witnesses to people they know and meet.

ARISE Together in Christ

ARISE Together in Christ is a three-year, parish-centered process of spiritual renewal and evangelization that enables people

to deepen their faith, develop a closer relationship with Christ, grow in community, and reach out in service to others. It emphasizes people living in good relationship with one another, as they make concrete applications of the Gospel to their life situations.

ARISE Together in Christ is a total renewal experience for the parish, spiritually transforming people through small Christian communities, special parish activities, reflections for families with teens and children, and Christian social action. There are five six-week seasons:

- Season One: **Encountering Christ Today**
- Season Two: **Change Our Hearts**
- Season Three: **In the Footsteps of Christ**
- Season Four: **New Heart, New Spirit**
- Season Five: **We Are the Good News!**

For each season, RENEW International offers a faith-sharing book and a music CD with the songs suggested in the faith-sharing book.

ARISE for youth

Faith-sharing materials for each session of all five seasons, written especially for youth. Also includes a separate *ARISE* for youth Leader Guide.

ARISE Family Sharing Pages

A friendly easy way to explore the same faith themes at home and in class. Four-page, full-color worksheet for each session of each Season. Available for Grades 1-3, and Grades 4-6.

WHY CATHOLIC?

Journey through the Catechism

WHY CATHOLIC? is a parish-based process of evangelization and adult faith formation. This process, designed for sharing in small Christian communities, is structured around exploring the important truths of our faith as they are presented in the *Catechism of the Catholic Church* and in the *United States Catholic Catechism for Adults.*

WHY CATHOLIC? helps nourish faith and enhance our sense of Catholic identity. The process and materials encourage us to understand and live the reasons why we are Catholic, and so lead us to a faith that is experienced more authentically, connecting us more deeply and meaningfully to God, and to others.

There are four books in the **WHY CATHOLIC?** series, each offering twelve sessions:

- PRAY: Christian Prayer
- BELIEVE: Profession of Faith
- CELEBRATE: Sacraments
- LIVE: Christian Morality

For each of the four **WHY CATHOLIC?** books, there is a **Song CD.** Each CD is a 12-song compilation of the songs suggested for the moments of prayer during the faith-sharing sessions. The CDs are available singly, or as a set.

For more information or to order these and other fine resources from **RENEW International**, please visit our secure online bookstore at **www.renewintl.org/store** or use our toll free order line: **1-888-433-3221.**

Did you know...?

RENEW International is a not-for-profit Catholic ministry organization that has touched the lives of 25 million people in the United States, Canada, and 22 other countries.

From the inner city and rural areas to remote parts of the developing world, **RENEW International's** priority is to serve all parishes who desire to renew their faith and build the Church, regardless of their economic situation.

Throughout **RENEW's** dynamic history, individuals have generously reached out to support our mission.

Please join us by making a donation to **RENEW International** at **www.renewintl.org/donate**

Interested in learning more about RENEW?

World RENEW, our free eNewsletter, covers interesting topics on today's spiritual life with behind-the-scenes stories and special features on **RENEW International's** work with parishes and small communities around the world.

To read more and explore how you can be an integral part of the **RENEW International** family, please visit **www.renewintl.org/subscribe**

Connect with us!

 facebook.com/RENEWIntl

 @RENEWIntl

 blog.renewintl.org

 youtube.com/RENEWInternational

NOTES

NOTES

NOTES

NOTES

NOTES

NOTES

NOTES

NOTES